WESTMAR COLLEGE  W9-APO-338

Selwyn Morgan

Cited in the *Congressional Record* and honored by the New York State legislature as a sports historian, **Harvey Frommer** is the author of more than twenty books on sports, mainly baseball. He was selected in a nationwide search to be the editor and principal author of the official book of the 1984 Olympics in Los Angeles. Frommer has a Ph.D. in Communications from New York University and teaches writing and speech at the City University of New York. He has recently collaborated on autobiographies of Red Holzman and Nolan Ryan.

LIBRARY

Books by **Harvey Frommer**

Primitive Baseball
Throwing Heat: The Autobiography of Nolan Ryan
Red on Red: The Autobiography of Red Holzman
Olympic Controversies
City Tech: The First 40 Years
Baseball's Greatest Managers
Baseball's Hall of Fame
The Games of the XXIIIrd Olympiad;
Los Angeles 1984: Official Commemorative Book
(Editor and Principal Author)
Jackie Robinson
Baseball's Greatest Records, Streaks, and Feats
Sports Genes (with Myrna Frommer)
Baseball's Great Rivalry:
The New York Yankees and the Boston Red Sox
Rickey and Robinson:
The Men Who Broke Baseball's Color Barrier
Basketball My Way (by Nancy Lieberman
with Harvey and Myrna Frommer)
The Sports Date Book (with Myrna Frommer)
New York City Baseball: 1947–1957
The Great American Soccer Book
Sports Roots
Sports Lingo: A Dictionary of the Language of Sports
The Martial Arts: Judo and Karate
A Sailing Primer
A Baseball Century

Primitive
Baseball

Primitive
Baseball

Primitive Baseball

The First Quarter-Century of the National Pastime

HARVEY FROMMER

88-1262

Atheneum   **1988**   NEW YORK

Photograph credit: *National Baseball Library*
                            Cooperstown, New York

The Publisher wishes to express appreciation to Thomas Heitz, librarian, and Patricia Kelly, photograph collection manager, National Baseball Library, for their research assistance with the photographs reproduced in this book.

Copyright © 1988 by Harvey Frommer

All rights reserved. No part of this book may be reproduced or transmitted in any form or by any means, electronic or mechanical, including photocopying, recording or by any information storage and retrieval system, without permission in writing from the Publisher.

Atheneum
Macmillan Publishing Company
866 Third Avenue, New York, N.Y. 10022
Collier Macmillan Canada, Inc.

Library of Congress Cataloging-in-Publication Data
Frommer, Harvey.
    Primitive baseball.

    1. Baseball—United States—History.   I. Title.
GV863.A1F76   1988   796.357'09   84-45708
ISBN 0-689-11567-9

Macmillan books are available at special discounts for bulk purchases for sales promotions, premiums, fund-raising, or educational use. For details, contact:

                Special Sales Director
                Macmillan Publishing Company
                866 Third Avenue
                New York, N.Y. 10022

10 9 8 7 6 5 4 3 2 1

Printed in the United States of America

For Gertrude Katz,
a love of a human being

The future of baseball is without limit. The time is coming when there will be great amphitheaters throughout the United States in which citizens shall be able to see the teams take part in the finest athletic struggles of the world.

—Albert G. Spalding

Contents

Contents

Primitive
Baseball

Primitive
Baseball

I
Roots

Mythology coats baseball history; some would say mythology lacquers baseball history. And although the myth that Abner Doubleday was the inventor of the sport has been repeatedly denigrated, he still is acknowledged in many quarters as the father of the national pastime.

The game's actual parent was Alexander Joy Cartwright, Jr., a descendant of British sea captains. In 1842 Cartwright, then twenty-two years old, was part of a group of young men from New York City's financial district who enjoyed playing "base ball" on a vacant lot on 27th Street and Fourth Avenue in Manhattan. Three years later, the group organized themselves into the Knickerbockers Base Ball Club, with a restricted membership of forty males and annual dues of five dollars.

And the following year, it was Cartwright who devised a brand-new set of rules and regulations for the game, including foul lines, nine players a side, and nine innings to a game. The rules also provided for a square infield—known as a diamond—ninety feet to a side, with a base at each corner. Punctuality for the players and the designation of an umpire to see that three strikes resulted in an out and that only three outs were allowed per side per inning also were included in the new rules.

"Soaking" or "plugging"—firing the ball at a runner to retire him, a painful practice—was eliminated. The rules stated: "A player running the bases shall be out if the ball is in the hands of an adversary on the base, or the runner is touched with it before he makes his bases; it being understood, however, that in no instance however is a ball to be thrown at him." Cartwright's rules also specified that a game ended when a team scored 21 "aces" or runs. And fielders produced outs by catching a batted ball on the first bounce, catching a ball on the fly in the air, tossing the ball to a base ahead of the runner, or tagging a runner out between bases.

With the new set of rules for the new game in place, the Knickerbockers, bedecked in white flannel shirts, blue woolen pantaloons, and spiffy straw hats, offered a challenge match to any team willing to test their mettle. The New York Nine provided the opposition in a game played on June 19, 1846, on an ancient cricket playground, Elysian Field in Hoboken, New Jersey. Lacking the playing services of their star player Cartwright, who functioned as the umpire, the Knickerbockers were routed 23–1 by the

4

New York Nine. And the first baseball game was in the record books.

Although Cartwright was the "father" of American baseball, he did not stay around long enough to see the growth of his child. On March 1, 1849, he left New York City and headed to California—one of hundreds of thousands lured by the discovery of gold. His diary notation of April 23, 1849, written in Independence, Missouri, a stopover on his way west, related the following:

"During the past week we have passed the time in fixing wagon-covers, stowing property, etc., varied by hunting and fishing and playing base ball. It is comical to see the mountain men and Indians playing the new game. I have the ball with me that we used back home [New York]."

Cartwright did not tarry long in California, for he was put off by the frenzy and fervor of those questing for gold. He settled down in Hawaii, where he died on July 13, 1892.

Baseball's Hall of Fame in 1939, acting on the findings of the Mills Commission—headed aptly enough by A. G. Mills—a group appointed to document baseball's origins, credited Abner Doubleday with creating the sport in 1839 at Cooperstown, New York. It was claimed that Doubleday laid out the first baseball diamond in a cow pasture in Cooperstown when he was a cadet at the United States Military Academy.

At this point Bruce Cartwright, who lived in Honolulu and was a grandson of Alexander Cartwright, entered the scene. Armed with his grandfather's diary, clippings, and other documents, he argued passionately that Alexander Cartwright, not Abner Doubleday, was the originator of baseball. Too much money and effort had been expended preparing to celebrate the "centennial" to call it off. As an accommodation, some would say as balm to soothe Bruce Cartwright, an Alexander Cartwright Day was included in the festivities that inaccurately celebrated Abner Doubleday as the man who invented baseball.

Cartwright's game—with its first written rules— was a "refined" version of "town ball," "goal ball," "baste ball," the "Massachusetts game," and other bat-and-ball sports, all of which derived from the English games of rounders and cricket.

A strict code of personal behavior characterized the atmosphere of those early baseball teams. Unlike the folk games—the pickup games that had preceded Cartwright's game—the new game was a stylized affair, a gentlemen's game. Only those spectators invited by the competing clubs bore witness to the early baseball games. Ladies were comfortably seated in the shade of tents; and tea, crackers, and other polite refreshments were made available for all spectators.

The purpose of the game was to allow the batter to hit; pitchers obliged by throwing the ball where the batter requested it. Bunting was frowned upon. Players trapped off base allowed themselves to be politely tagged out. Unruliness on the part of players was discouraged; fines were levied against players who disobeyed their captain, argued with the umpire, or resorted to profanity.

Home teams would treat visiting teams to a gala dinner after games, and social gatherings between clubs that included wives and girl friends highlighted the off-season. Baseball was indeed a game for gentlemen. It was also a restricted game for a time—limited to amateurs and the upper social class.

In 1858 the National Association of Base Ball Players (NABBP) was organized. Basically consisting of some fifty teams from the East, the NABBP attempted to keep the genteel climate of the game in force and barred professionals and those players who were deemed not to be of the right social standing. Some but not all of the NABBP teams even refused to compete against clubs they regarded as their social inferiors. However, the most telling change in the state of organized baseball was revealed in the fact that not one of the NABBP's six original officers was a representative of Cartwright's old Knickerbocker club.

The Excelsiors of Brooklyn in 1860 were the first club to go on the road, trimming teams in Baltimore, Wilmington, and Philadelphia. More than 3,000 fans crowded about to watch the Excelsiors, a team that did much to publicize baseball. Nineteen-year-old Jim Creighton was their star. The first pitcher who harnessed speed and control, Creighton also threw a pitch described as curveball.

By the late 1850s, baseball had become more democratized and was daily increasing in popularity against its main rival, cricket, whose slowness and lengthy playing time doomed it as a major American sport. Unlike cricket, baseball, in Mark Twain's words, was "the very symbol, the outward and visible expression of the drive and push and rush and struggle of the raging, tearing, booming nineteenth century."

Fans—they were called "cranks"—engaged in all types of outrageous behavior: heckling umpires, razzing players, even rioting. For the fans, it was suggested, baseball was not simply a matter of life and death—it was more important than that. The final stanza of "Casey at the Bat" epitomized the emotional pull of the sport:

> Oh! somewhere in this favored land
>   the sun is shining bright;
> The band is playing somewhere,
>   and somewhere hearts are light.
> And somewhere men are laughing,
>   and somewhere children shout
> But there is no joy in Mudville—
>   mighty Casey has Struck Out.

Even the great catastrophe of the Civil War did not impede the growth of baseball. In fact, the sport was spurred on by it. On Christmas Day in 1862, approximately 40,000 troops watched baseball games. In prison camps, Union prisoners passed the time by playing baseball and even challenged their Confederate captors in contests of baseball skill. After the war, returning veterans brought back their zeal and zest for the game to hamlets, little towns, farm areas. Albert Spalding, for one, was tutored in the intricacies of the game in 1863 by a veteran in his hometown of Rockford, Illinois.

Postwar baseball boomed, but it was also rife with scandal. In 1866 the Philadelphia Athletics openly paid three players $20 a week; many other players were on payrolls in a more disguised manner. One egregious example of this practice was engaged in by Tammany Hall boss William Marcy Tweed, president of the New York Mutuals from 1860 to 1871. All his baseball players were classified as sweepers or clerks on the New York City payroll—a classification that cost the taxpayers of New York City $30,000 annually.

"Hippodroming" of games became the vogue in some quarters. That was the practice of players consorting with gamblers to fix scores or games. At some ball parks, gamblers were out in the open quoting odds, taking bets, collecting money. The Troy (New York) Haymakers were reportedly under the total control of gamblers. Six-shooters were fired in games in California just as a fielder was about to camp under a fly ball. The guns, it was understood, were on the side of the team that was batting. In some games where much money had been wagered, fans flocked out onto the field to prevent a loss to the team they had backed with their pocketbooks.

"So common has betting become," noted *Harper's Weekly*, "that the most respectable clubs in the country indulge in it to a highly culpable degree, and so common . . . the tricks by which games have been 'sold' for the benefit of gamblers that the most respectable participants have been suspected of baseness."

"Revolving" was another problem that drew daily criticism from the newspapers of the time. It was a

9

practice that witnessed players moving from team to team—in effect, selling their services to the highest bidder. One notorious example was the case of William Fischer. Agreeing to perform for the Philadelphia Athletics after being rewarded by the team with a brand-new suit of clothes, a job, room and board, and a fifteen-dollar bonus, Fischer left the team in the lurch after a few days. He then "revolved" with his new suit and his bonus money to the Cubs of Chicago, who had offered a better deal for his services.

By 1860 recruitment of players by teams and revolving were an established part of the game scene. Players like James Creighton, Al Reach, Arthur Cummings, and Joe Start became heroes; more and more fans came to the ball parks to see these attractions in action. By the final years of the 1860s, "professionals" were on the rosters of most of the leading teams of the day: the Haymakers, the Brooklyn Atlantics, the Mutuals, the Athletics, the Chicago White Stockings, the Lansingburgh (New York) Unions, the Buckeyes of Cincinnati, and the Marylands of Baltimore.

Baseball became more and more the American game, a sport played throughout the length and breadth of the country, a game that famed orator Clarence Darrow mused about when recalling his growing-up years in a small town in Ohio as "the one unalloyed joy in life."

Heated rivalries between eastern and western teams accentuated the excitement of baseball during the 1860s. Frenetic sectional competition was personified by the Washington Nationals of 1867, who in their tour of the West humbled all the teams they encountered. Then Washington arrived in Chicago to oppose the Forest City Club of Rockford, Illinois. Upholding western pride, Forest City, behind the pitching of young Albert Spalding, outlasted Washington 29–23 in the game played at Dexter Park. Watches, jewelry, and other gifts were bestowed on the Rockford nine by the town's grateful citizens. The celebration and merriment went on for more than a week and were finally brought to an end when the Washington Nationals issued an open letter offering the disclaimer that they were not the national champions.

Washington and Forest City and the other teams of the time, however, were merely pretenders to the throne of the best baseball team of that era. In the offing loomed an aggregation from the Queen City of Cincinnati—the Red Stockings.

"THE FIRST PROFESSIONAL BASEBALL TEAM"

The Cincinnati Red Stockings of 1869 are storied in legend as baseball's first professional team, but other nonamateur teams preceded the Cincinnati club. The Red Stockings, however, were the first team to trot across America with its players signed to contracts binding them to a club for an entire season. In short, though the Red Stockings were not the first professional team, their real claim to fame is as the first all-salaried team.

Organized in 1867 and then reorganized in 1869

by twenty-six-year-old attorney Aaron B. Champion, the Cincinnati team was entrusted to the hands of English-born Harry Wright, a former jeweler and cricket player, a veteran of a decade of top-drawer baseball competition. Champion looked upon the Red Stockings as a way to promote the city of Cincinnati and its products and services. And Champion looked upon Harry Wright as scout, recruiter, player, and manager—as a man to get a job done.

The Red Stockings were referred to as a "picked nine," which might have been an exaggeration—but it was a nine picked by Harry Wright. The only native of Cincinnati on the team was first baseman Charlie Gould, nicknamed the "bushel basket" because of his ability to snare baseballs. Others included Wright, his brother George, star shortstop, obtained from the Morrisania Unions of New York; third baseman Fred Waterman; outfielders Asa Brainard, Dave Birdsall, and Andy Leonard; pitcher Cal McVey; second baseman Cal Sweasy; catcher Doug Allison. Harry Wright doubled as a relief pitcher, and Dick Hurley, appropriated from the Buckeyes of Cincinnati, functioned as a utility player. Harry Wright was the pride of Cincinnati. On his wedding day fans gave him a gold watch wrapped in a $100 government bond and his twelve teammates presented him with an inscribed gold medal.

The team's total payroll for the 1869 season was $9,300. Salaries covered the period from March to November and ranged from $800 to $1,400 for the nine starters—the lone sub picked up $600.

12

Wright was a strict disciplinarian, a smart baseball man, and a shrewd promoter. He decreed that his team was to wear bright red stockings to set off their white flannel shirts and pants and dark Oxford shoes. Some criticized the style of garb as garish. It may have been a bit outlandish for that time, but the red stockings did attract attention and that was what Wright and Champion were in the game for.

Wright's team was prepared to take on all comers—the price was right—the Queen City team pocketed a hefty share of the gate receipts.

Winners of their first seventeen games, the team from the West confronted the Mutuals on June 14, 1869, before 8,000 fans at the Union Grounds in Brooklyn. The Red Stockings prevailed 4–2 over the tough eastern team. The victory was a pivotal moment in the fortunes of the Red Stockings, for from that triumph on opponents realized the Cincinnati team was not a side show but a main event.

That season the Cincinnati Red Stockings played baseball throughout the Northeast and West, traveled 11,000 miles, thanks to the new transcontinental railroad. The team won 57 games and recorded one disputed tie against the Troy Haymakers. Over 23,000 spectators witnessed their six-game series in New York City and almost 15,000 assembled for a game in Philadelphia. The team had a private audience in Washington with President Ulysses S. Grant, who complimented the western "Cinderella" club for its skills and winning ways.

Photographs of the "picked nine," serious-looking

young men with beards and sideburns, were everywhere. The stock photographs captured the facade but not the tone of the team. Excessive alcohol consumption, a penchant for skipping practices and missing trains, and an eccentric and individualistic attitude characterized the merry band of players, who swept the country, along with their theme song:

We are a band of baseball players
From Cincinnati city.
We come to toss the ball around
And sing to you our ditty
And if you listen to the song
We are about to sing,
We'll tell you all about baseball
And make the welkin ring.
The ladies want to know
Who are those gallant men in
Stockings red, they'd like to know.

Feted and praised in a lavish homecoming, the Red Stockings were presented with a twenty-seven-foot bat by the Cincinnati Lumber Company—a symbol of their on-the-field accomplishments. "I'd rather be president of the Cincinnati Baseball Club," bragged Champion, "than president of the United States."

"Glory," one proud Cincinnati booster said, "I don't know anything about baseball or town ball, nowadays, but it does me good to see those fellows. They've done something to add to the glory of our city. They advertised the city, advertised us, sir, and helped our business."

Although the Red Stockings helped many busi-

14

nesses and although their fame was fabled, after all salaries and expenses had been laid out the club was in the red in more ways than one. The team's net profit in 1869 was a puny $1.39. For although the Red Stockings had some big paydays in New York City and Philadelphia, there were washouts figuratively and literally in other places. Sawdust and brooms applied to the wet places on the field in Rochester sopped up rainy day problems there. But in Syracuse Wright's baseballers had to contend with a ball park ready for the wrecker's ball: twelve-inch-high grass, and a live-pigeon shoot being staged on the field. Syracuse was a nonpayday.

Nevertheless, in the final balance sheet of baseball doings for 1869, the Red Stockings of Cincinnati managed to have a tremendous impact on the state of baseball in America. "They met with such remarkable success in that year," noted famed baseball journalist Harry Chadwick, "that their exploits are noteworthy in the history of the game."

Part of the impact of the Red Stockings was on other cities that wanted a baseball champion to represent them. Cincinnati's success made it sunset time for the amateur in baseball and dawn for professionalism.

An editorial in the Chicago *Tribune*, miffed because it was constantly reporting on the one-sided losses of the local team, reflected the mood of the time. It called for "a representative club; an organization as great as her [Chicago's] enterprise and wealth, one that will not allow the second-rate clubs of every village in the Northwest to carry away the honors in baseball."

The Red Stockings had triggered a trend. In Chicago, civic pride enabled $20,000 to be raised to organize a strong professional team, and advertisements were placed soliciting the efforts of topflight players. In other cities the same type of enterprising effort was launched. Teams that had previously competed wearing the mask of amateurism now would become full-fledged professional organizations.

The following season the Red Stockings kept right on rolling over the opposition. Their streak reached 92 straight wins, 27 in a row out of the gate in 1870. Then on June 14, 1870, at the Capitoline Grounds in Brooklyn, they lost 8–7 as the Atlantics scored three runs in the bottom of the eleventh inning.

Incredibly, the defeat destroyed some of the mystique of the Red Stockings; jaded fans did not flock to games as they previously had. Then the Red Stockings experienced another defeat—this time to Chicago. Champion was forced out of the presidency by a revolt of Cincinnati stockholders, and penny pinching became the order of the day as a buffer against declining attendance. With money tight, with Champion still on the scene but without power, the Wright brothers, Harry and George, moved on with some of the best Cincinnati players and later set up shop in Boston in the National Association of Professional Baseball Players. It was there they would inaugurate another baseball dynasty—the Boston Red Stockings. That 1870 season was the last hurrah for the Cincin-

16

nati Red Stockings. Before the year was over, the club broke up. Every player from the '69 team caught on with clubs in the new National Association. The NABBP would tarry for a while as a viable entity and then time and progress would pass it by.

The National Association was founded on March 17, 1871—St. Patrick's Day—at Collier's Cafe on Broadway and 13th Street in New York City. The organization's charter members included the Red Stockings, Chicago White Stockings, Cleveland Forest Citys, Fort Wayne Kekiongas, New York Mutuals, Philadelphia Athletics, Rockford Forest Citys, Washington Nationals, and Washington Olympics. The Eckfords of Brooklyn attended the meeting but declined to participate that first National Association season, not wishing to chance losing the ten-dollar admission fee. When the Kekiongas dropped out of the league in midsummer, the Eckfords took their place. A 22–7 record enabled the Philadelphia Athletics to win the first National Association championship. Chicago took second place. The Red Stockings, hampered by injuries, wound up third in 1871.

However, from 1872 to 1875 Wright's Red Stockings won three championships and utterly dominated the National Association. One of the great stars Harry Wright could always rely on was his younger brother George. A bushy-mustached 150-pounder filled with verve and baseball skills, George batted .409, .336, .378, .345, and .337 with Boston. He was one of the major reasons for the Red Stockings' success.

Another even more significant reason for Boston's winning ways was pitcher Albert Goodwill Spalding, possessor of a herky-jerk underhand delivery out of which came fast ball after fast ball. In five seasons with Boston, Spalding won 207 games, lost just 56. In 1875 his record was an eye-popping 57–5.

Wright's team was a colossus astride the National Association. In 1875, the Red Stockings posted an incredible 71–8 record and lost just one game on their home field. That 1875 season the top four hitters in the National Association were from Boston; eight of the top twenty batters were Red Stockings. Only Harry Wright averaged less than a hit a game that year, and he was almost washed up. With Albert Spalding holding the other teams down and with Boston batters racking up opposing pitchers, it was no contest. The Red Stockings finished 15 games ahead of the pack.

Other teams in the league were hapless. Just five of them played at a .500 clip that 1875 season. The Brooklyn team was a joke with a 2 and 42 record; Keokuk, Iowa, managed just one triumph in 13 games and left the league. Four other teams combined for a record of 17–88 and also dropped out of the National Association.

Afflicted with domination by the Red Stockings, a team that demoralized and unbalanced competition (the National Association was called Harry Wright's league); with heavy drinking by many players (it was called lushing even back then); with the throwing of games (hippodroming); with players moving at will from team to team (revolving); with few

18

clubs actually making money and others simply refusing to complete their schedules—the five-year-old league saw twenty-five different clubs come and go; with a total lack of leadership, the National Association was a mess.

That mess set the stage for William A. Hulbert. In 1870 he had become a charter stockholder of the Chicago White Stockings of the National Association. "I'd rather be a lamppost in Chicago," he had bragged, "then a millionaire elsewhere. I'll take control of this game of baseball away from the easterners."

When Boston made its first trip to Chicago in 1875, Hulbert, poised to become club president, arranged a private meeting with the highly successful but also highly ambitious Albert Spalding.

"You've no business playing in Boston," Hulbert informed Spalding. "You're a western boy and should be playing here. If you come to Chicago, you can be captain and manager of the team at $4,000 a year and I'll take over the presidency and we'll give those easterners the fight of their lives."

The idea appealed to Spalding. Although he was a big star in Boston, he was a man always anxious to better his station in life. "You bet, I'll come to Chicago," Spalding told Hulbert. "And I'll bring a team of pennant winners along with me—Ross Barnes, Cal McVey, and Deacon White. The people call us the Big Four, but the owners don't pay us very well. A championship team should be paid like champions."

The Big Four announced their plans to the fury

of the cranks of Boston. "You seceders," some of the unhappy fans screamed. "Your White Stockings will get soiled in Chicago."

Hulbert, never afraid of being called an over-reacher, also signed the young Philadelphia phenom Cap Anson to a contract for 1876. And with the "Big Four" and Anson in the fold, William Ambrose Hulbert was primed for battle.

So were National Association moguls miffed by all of Hulbert's maneuverings. They began to set plans in motion to eject the Chicagoan and his White Stockings from the league. The resourceful Hulbert arranged a meeting with Spalding to plan a counterattack strategy.

"Mr. Hulbert and I were in a serious discussion about what we should do," Spalding recalled. "For a few moments I noticed that he was engrossed in deep thought. 'Spalding, I have a new scheme. Let us anticipate the eastern cusses and organize a new association before the March meeting, and then we shall see who shall do the expelling.' "

On February 2, 1876, a great storm lashed the Atlantic seaboard. A seventy-mile-an-hour gale ravaged the New York City area and business was brought to a standstill. Most people stayed at home.

William A. Hulbert of Chicago was a long way from home. He peered out the window of his room at the fashionable Grand Central Hotel in Manhattan and contemplated the fury of nature. The president of the Chicago baseball team of the National Association had traveled to New York City to meet with four easterners to convince them of the great sporting and financial future of baseball, a future he believed was there for the taking if they would only go along with his vision.

A month before in Louisville, the ambitious and flamboyant forty-four-year-old Hulbert had met secretly with representatives of St. Louis, Cincinnati, and Louisville. He had convinced them of the wisdom of forming a new baseball league that would stem what he called the decline of the game.

While the wind howled and steeples fell in New York City, Hulbert first shrewdly conferred privately for a half hour with representatives of each of the eastern clubs. Then he gathered together the entire aggregation in a second-floor meeting room in the Grand Central Hotel.

With great theatrical flourish, Hulbert went to the door once all the representatives were settled. He turned the key in the lock and then made a great show of depositing it in his pocket.

"Do not be alarmed, gentlemen." He smiled. "I merely took the precaution of seeing that there will not be any intrusion from the outside. There is some business that has to be finished and no one will leave this room until I have explained everything."

The easterners representing Boston, Hartford, New York City, and Philadelphia listened as Hulbert patiently explained that he had been granted the power of attorney from the four western clubs to create a new baseball organization. Then he launched into a bitter tirade about the low state of baseball. A

21

businessman who had never played baseball, Hulbert was appalled at the player-controlled state of the National Association of Professional Baseball Players, a league that was run largely by the players.

"Inflated salaries," Hulbert continued, telling the eastern representatives what they knew well, "players jumping from team to team during the season, gambling scandals, team imbalance, incomplete schedules—all of these can and will be wiped away."

Hulbert was not just holding forth but was accurately outlining many of the vexing problems of National Association baseball: teams located in cities of different sizes, creating disjointed demographics from which to draw. No specific schedule of games. Heavy gambling action and bookmakers flourishing with their booths out in the open. Players allegedly fixing games for the right price. Fracases, fights, and near riots sometimes accompanying the baseball action.

"I propose"—Hulbert spoke in a loud and impassioned voice—"a closed corporation" of baseball. "Why should we be losing money when we represent a game that people love?"

The men whom Hulbert had once disparagingly referred to as "eastern cusses" agreed with his complaints and reasoning. They told him to go on with his presentation. Hulbert explained that the new league he envisioned would be called the National League of Professional Base Ball Clubs. In an age of Carnegie, Rockefeller, Vanderbilt, Gould, that name was appropriate. It would be a league of clubs—not players.

For the first time baseball would become a management-labor situation, with club owners and administrators running the show and players now cast in the role of employees.

Hulbert had caught the easterners off guard when he locked the door on them. Now he astonished them when he unveiled a thirteen-point constitution and a player's contract for the new league. Both had been created by Hulbert and Albert Spalding, a businessman as well as an athlete, who looked upon the formation of the new league as a way to give management the upper hand—in his phrase—"in the irrepressible conflicts between Labor and Capital."

Constitutional objectives of the new league were "first, to encourage, foster and elevate the game of baseball; second, to enact and enforce proper rules for the exhibition and conduct of the game; third, to make base ball playing respectable and honorable."

At the heart of the constitution was the principle that baseball be a profit-making venture; the day of the sport operating as a hobby for status-seeking gentlemen belonged in the past, in Hulbert's view.

Agreement was reached on "territorial rights" —the establishment of but one franchise representing a city of at least 75,000 in population. League members were banned from competing against non-league teams. New applicants for a franchise would have to be voted in by current club owners and two "blackballs would bar an applicant."

All teams would be required to complete their entire league schedule. Annual dues would be $100—

23

ten times the amount assessed by the old National Association. To promote and enhance a lofty and moral image, the constitution specified that Sunday baseball was prohibited, sale of alcohol would not be allowed on clubs' grounds, and gambling of any sort would be illegal. Provisions were also made for police protection. Players would not be permitted to fraternize with fans, and unruly spectators would be subject to ejection from the ball park by the umpire.

The transfer of power from the players to the owners was the most revolutionary aspect of the constitution. Players would now be tightly bound to their clubs. The lessons of the past—of athletes moving about by whim or responding to the price of the highest bidder—had been painfully absorbed. The Boston Red Stockings, for example, had became a highly successful National Association club by stocking its roster with the best available talent because it paid the highest salaries—about $2,000 per player, a hefty sum for those days.

Additional National League constitutional provisions gave a club the power to expel a player from the league and to create a new type of contract, requiring players to be accountable to all rules laid down by the club. In effect, the constitution was a blank check for the owners providing them with total control of the management, regulation, and resolution of every possible dispute.

Other modern features of the new National League, aimed at making the game of professional baseball less rowdy and more organized, included provisions

24

for paying umpires five dollars a game, for permitting only the captain of a team to dispute an umpire's decisions, for scheduling games, and for setting uniform admission prices.

In an age of big business growth the new league was in step with the times. Although its structure was primitive, the National League would nevertheless persevere and set a precedent for all sports teams of the twentieth century. In theory and in practice the National League would be a loosely organized cartel—a closed corporation designed to restrict competition among other franchises for players. In essence, the aim of the National League of Professional Base Ball Clubs was to become the only game in town.

William Ambrose Hulbert had a good head for figures and explained to the eastern representatives that the new league would play a highly organized seventy-game schedule. The eight charter National League clubs would be Chicago, Boston, New York, Philadelphia, Hartford, Cincinnati, St. Louis, and Louisville. Each of these teams would play 10 games against every other team. The one that won the most games would win the championship and an emblem of victory—a flag. That pennant would cost no more than $100, but it would symbolize the National League champ.

After the eastern representatives approved the thirteen points of the new National League constitution, a five-man committee was elected to run the league. A well-known politician, Morgan G. Bulkeley of Hartford, was chosen as president after Hulbert declined the post and supported the Connecticut man.

Then Hulbert prevailed on each delegate to sign a statement that denigrated the National Association for insidious abuses "growing out of an imperfect and unsystematized code." The last order of business was a notice sent out to newspapers after the day-long meeting at the Grand Central Hotel. The notice declared that eight teams had withdrawn from the National Association and had formed the National League of Professional Base Ball Clubs. Although a significant event in the history of sports had taken place, three days passed before one of the New York City morning newspapers reported what had taken place. Under the heading "Sporting," the news of the new league was preceded by a paragraph about the cancellation of the Savannah Jockey Club's races of the previous day and a report on pigeon shooting lengthier than the news about the new league.

History marks the year 1876 as an American centennial, a time when Ulysses S. Grant was president, when P. T. Barnum was all the rage, when Alexander Graham Bell invented the telephone. It was also the time when the National League came full flower into the world.

The new league was not an altruistic endeavor created by a few honorable men to salvage the sport of baseball, to transform it into the true national pastime and make it "respectable." It was a power play on the part of Hulbert—a self-serving economic power play that worked magnificently. Professional baseball players were totally taken by surprise and so was the National Association. At a March meeting the

26

old league attempted to fight back, to reorganize. The efforts were not successful, and the National Association faded into history.

Newspapers debated the fate of the failed National Association and the merits of the new league. Eastern publications, especially those from towns the National League had chosen to pass over, attacked Hulbert.

The Chicago *Tribune*, not totally unbiased where Hulbert was concerned, had dispatched a writer to cover the meeting of moguls in the Grand Central Hotel. The writer had the inside track on all other scribes. His publication featured his report, some would say "puff piece," on the wheelings and dealings by Hulbert and his new cronies under the headline: THE DIAMOND SQUARED. The writer also uncharitably characterized famed baseball scribe Harry Chadwick as "the Old Man of the Sea . . . a dead weight on the neck of the game."

Chadwick, no stranger to journalistic skirmishes, responded in the New York *Clipper* wondering why the new National League had utilized what he called cloak-and-dagger means to achieve a moral end. "Reform should not fear the light of day," wrote Chadwick, continuing that the new league was "a sad blunder . . . a star-chamber method of attaining . . . objects." He suggested that it would have been fairer to have proffered invitations to all existing professional teams.

The St. Louis *Dispatch* questioned the morality that the operators of the new National League claimed as a cornerstone of their enterprise. The Phillies, the *Dispatch* pointed out, were not welcomed into the National League because of the record of gambling that had attached itself to that club. However, the Mutuals of New York were admitted to the new enterprise despite their record of dishonest play. The writer of the *Dispatch* article therefore concluded that the highly lucrative New York–area demographics meant more to the National League than the reform morality they professed.

In Chicago, Albert Goodwill Spalding, premier exponent of the underhand delivery, who had pitched the Boston team to four straight pennants from 1872 to 1875 and would become Hulbert's lieutenant as player-manager of the White Stockings, told the *Tribune*: "championship matches will draw a better average attendance . . . the public will feel confident that strong men will meet."

The *Tribune* also reported that Spalding would open "a large emporium in Chicago where he will sell all kinds of baseball goods and turn his place into the headquarters for the Western ball clubs." Spalding's players would be garbed in uniforms from the sturdy shelves of his shop. He would produce a different colored cap for each player's position, making the team resemble, in the *Tribune*'s phrase, "a Dutch bed of tulips."

For Spalding, life then was a bed of roses. The new league granted him a monopoly to supply the official baseballs and a license to publish its official guide.

Life was not as fragrant an enterprise for the new National League players. Almost totally controlled by the owners, made to pay for their own uniforms, the players were also required to donate fifty cents a day each in expense money for road trips. These charges made players complain, but their protests were to no avail. Ignored by the owners, the players were attacked in some newspapers as being an over-pampered lot. Fifty cents was a handy sum back then— that was also the admission price to National League games, although fans arriving after the third inning could gain access to the baseball doings for a dime.

That first National League season of 1876 was thirty years removed from "the first baseball game" ever played in the United States on June 19, 1846, on Elysian Field in Hoboken, New Jersey, a short ferry ride across the Hudson River. In those three decades between the first baseball game and the first National League game, a myriad of changes had taken place in the sport that would become the national pastime, and more transformations were in the offing.

II
The National League and Its Competitors

The original eight National League franchises included Chicago, managed by Al Spalding; St. Louis, led by Herman Dehlman; Hartford, piloted by Bob Ferguson; Louisville, skippered by Chick Fulmer; Philadelphia, handled by Al Wright; Cincinnati, led by Charlie Gould; Boston, managed by Harry Wright; and New York, piloted by Bill Cammeyer.

The first game in the history of the National League took place on April 22, 1876. Boston opposed Philadelphia. Little note was taken of the event by Philadelphia journalists; a few lines in fine print were published in Philadelphia newspapers:

The championship season of 1876 was opened on Saturday afternoon by the Boston and Athletic [sic], on the grounds of Twenty-fifth and Jefferson streets. As was anticipated there was a large turnout to witness the game, which was well worth seeing, both nines being in full force. The first inning was a blank for both clubs, although O'Rourke for the Boston and Fisler and Meyerle for the Athletic made clean hits, the latter's being a two-baser.

The Athletics should have won the game but their fielding was poor. Sutton, at third, was particularly miserable, and had to be transferred. The batting of the home nine, however, was superior to that of Boston. Great interest was manifested in the event as it was really the first game of importance of the season.

Boston . . . . 0 1 2 0 1 0 0 0 2 —6
Athletics . . . 0 1 0 0 0 3 0 0 1 —5
Runs earned—Boston, Athletics, 2. First base on errors—Boston, 6. Athletics, 3. Bases on called balls—Boston, 2. Athletics, 1. Double plays—Eggler and Coons; Force, Fouser, and Fisler. Time of game 2 hours, 45 minutes.

The first batter in the history of the National League was George Wright. Designated as the leadoff batter for Boston by his brother Harry, George became a footnote to baseball history when he was retired on a ground ball to shortstop. "Orator Jim" O'Rourke of Boston recorded the first hit in National League history.

The winning pitcher in the first National League game was Joe Borden. Then, strangely, the twenty-two-year-old Borden, possessor of a 12–12 record, was dropped by Boston before the season was concluded. He hung on and completed the season working as a groundskeeper for Boston, but he never again pitched in a National League game.

31

On Monday April 24, 1876, Boston and Philadelphia played the second game of their series, and
surprisingly the press gave that contest much more
recognition. The account of the game was under the
heading "Baseball," and a box score and the name
of the umpire were included in the reportage.

The "Boston and Athletic Clubs" played their second game at 25th and Jefferson Streets yesterday afternoon in the presence of about 2,000 people. The weather
was disagreeable for ball playing and the spectators,
wrapped up in overcoats, resorted to outbursts of ap-
plause at frequent intervals to keep their blood above
the freezing point.

The Athletics, losing the toss, went to bat first, and
from the start to the close of the game, outbatted and
outfielded their opponents. Josephs, the pitcher of the
Boston nine, was hit with ease, while the Red Stockings
were unsuccessful in mastering Knight's delivery.

In consequence of the crippled condition of Sutton's right arm, a change was made in the positions of
the field of the Philadelphia nine: Sutton playing first-
base, Fisler at second-base and Meyerle at third-base.
Morrill was substituted for Parks on the Boston nine.

Staggered home starts were another feature of
that first National League season. Big league baseball
began in St. Louis on May 5, 1876, at the Grand
Avenue Grounds, before an estimated crowd of 3,000.
An account of that event reported:

The newly formed National League of Professional
Baseball Clubs played its first game in this city today
when the local St. Louis entry engaged the Chicago

nine. The efforts of the local team were rewarded with a 1–0 victory. Bradley, the St. Louis pitcher, gave up two hits and also made two of the seven hits St. Louis collected against the Chicago pitcher, Spalding.

George Washington Bradley would pitch the first no-hitter in National League history against Hartford on July 15, and wind up the season with a 45–19 record—the same record as his St. Louis team—but Bradley's sterling efforts would not be enough to match Albert Goodwill Spalding and the Chicago White Stockings. The day of the four- or five-man rotation and the relief pitcher belonged to the future. Back then hurlers pitched almost all of their team's games.

That loss to St. Louis by Spalding and Chicago was just one of a meager total of 14 in 1876 for the White Stockings, who won 52 games. Many of the victories were by shutouts, and being "Chicagoed" or "whitewashed" became synonyms for a no-runs-scored loss to the White Stockings.

Rolling past most of their opposition, the Windy City team won the first pennant in National League history. Spalding dazzled and befuddled hitters, winning 47 games to lead the league. And eastern team "escapees" Cap Anson, Deacon White, Ross Barnes, and Cal McVey made major contributions to the efforts of the White Stockings. Barnes, capitalizing on the "fair-foul" hit (all a ball had to do at that time was be in fair territory for any part of its trajectory), batted a league-leading .429. First baseman McVey recorded a .347 average and also won five of the six games he

33

pitched when Al Spalding, manager and super hurler, decided to rest his arm and play a little first base.

Chicago scored 88 runs in a span of four straight games in July, setting a record that has never been topped, although it was a mark set when fielders went bare-handed after a ball. And on September 26, 1876, Chicago clinched the first pennant in National League history by trimming Hartford 7–6.

"They won," declared the Chicago *Tribune*, "and now, despite every combination, every abuse, every unfairness, they have played themselves fairly to the front, and so cleanly that nothing can throw off the grip they have on the flag."

Hartford did win nine games in a row near the end of the season, but it was too small a winning streak, too late in the chase.

Once again the Chicago *Tribune* served up lavish praise for the hometown team, lauding "Captain Spalding" for the heroic efforts that made the White Stockings work efficiently as a team while denigrating others, to whom the newspaper referred as "some gangs of quarrelsome bummers."

The city of Chicago was so swept away by the success of the White Stockings that plans were set in motion to replace horsecars with steamcars on the transit route to the park in 1877—"an easy accommodation for businessmen to facilitate their being able to save time to do extra work on days they wished to go to the ball park," according to one newspaper article of the day.

All things considered, the first National League season was a fairly successful one, despite the domination of the White Stockings; the futility of the hapless Cincinnati Red Stockings, who managed just 5 wins as opposed to 56 losses; and the failure to complete the season's schedule by the Philadelphia Athletics and the New York Mutuals, who balked at making their final western trips, claiming they were economically strapped and could not afford to spend any more money.

William A. Hulbert replaced Morgan G. Bulkeley, who resigned as league president. At the December annual meeting of the National League, Hulbert demanded and received a unanimous vote to expel the wayward Mutuals and Athletics, even though they represented the league's two biggest cities. Both teams would be kept out of the league until Hulbert's death in 1882.

No replacements were named for the Mutuals and Athletics, and the league moved into the 1877 season with six franchises. One outcome of the expulsion of the two teams was the creation of a uniform playing schedule that the entire league was required to adhere to. It was a brilliant idea that made the game of baseball even more ceremonious. Now fans and newspaper reporters would know in advance the dates of all "home" and "away" games played by teams. With the creation of two minor leagues—the International Association and the League Alliance—that 1877 season also saw the beginning of an organized baseball structure.

Hulbert continued to hold sway over the National League with a kind of ruthlessness. On October 30, 1877, four players on Louisville were expelled from baseball for life for "crooked play." It was alleged that each of the Louisville players had received $100 a game from implicated gamblers.

A not so hidden agenda that impinged on players was the "blacklist," a policy the National League had in force from its inception. The blacklist enabled a team to release or discharge a player, no matter the reason. Other teams then went along with the unwritten code of refusing to negotiate for that released player's services. More and more the blacklist became a weapon of the owners. At one stage in the early 1880s, thirty-four players and one umpire fell victim to it.

Several rivals challenged the establishment National League, but none could effectively break its monopoly in the nineteenth century. The American Association was the most successful of the rival leagues. Lasting from 1882 to 1891, the Association charged only twenty-five cents a ticket—half the admissions fee of the National League. Sunday baseball was allowed, as well as the sale of liquor at games. Charter franchises included Baltimore, Cincinnati, Louisville, Philadelphia, Pittsburgh, and St. Louis. Four of the six directors of those franchises owned breweries. Thus, the N.L. attacked the Association as a "beer and whiskey league."

It was actually the issue of beer that had triggered the creation of the American Association. In 1881 the National League objected to the Cincinnati team's selling beer in its ball park. Worcester was the biggest complainer among the National League teams and insisted that the Reds discontinue their "distasteful practice." The entire city of "Old Zinzinnati" was outraged at the antibeer stand, and a Cincy newspaper reflected the militant mood: "Puritanical Worcester is not liberal Cincinnati by a jugful and what is sauce for Worcester is wind for the Queen City. Beer and Sunday amusements have become a popular necessity in Cincinnati."

W. H. Kennett, president of the Cincinnati club, was adamant on the drinking issue and informed his colleagues in the National League that they could take Cincinnati with beer or not at all. It was not at all.

Miffed but anxious to get even, Cincinnati called together delegates from cities excluded from the National League and on November 2, 1881, formed the American Association of Base Ball Clubs. Charter members were Brooklyn, Cincinnati, Louisville, Pittsburgh, and St. Louis. Baltimore later replaced Brooklyn and Philadelphia joined the Association prior to the first season in 1882.

The new league went to war against the older circuit and extended invitations to National League players to become part of the American Association. Several players jumped leagues, prompting court battles and bitter diatribes between principals of both organizations.

The American Association had many appealing features besides Sunday baseball, the sale of liquor at the ball park, a twenty-five-cent admissions price compared to fifty cents for the National League. The American Association had a greater population in its six cities to draw from than the (at that time) eight-team National League. It also inaugurated a percentage system to determine pennant winners. Back then it was an innovative and even controversial gesture; now team standings based on won and lost percentages are commonplace in all sports.

Cincinnati won the first association pennant and began play against the Chicago White Sox, the National League pennant winner, in a postseason competition. The series, however, was stopped after two games had been played when the Association president threatened to expel the Reds for playing baseball with the "enemy."

In the midst of all the acrimony and hostility of the time the man who some referred to as the "father of the National League" died. William Hulbert succumbed to heart problems on April 10, 1882. Two days later Albert Spalding was among those who helped lower Hulbert's coffin into the ground. Spalding moved on to become president of the Chicago team, bought out Hulbert's holdings in the club, and assumed principal ownership along with John Walsh, a prominent Chicago banker.

Interleague warfare escalated early in 1883 when weak franchises in Troy and Worcester were dropped by the National League and replaced by New York and Philadelphia. The N.L. plan was for these franchises to go head-to-head against the Association teams in those cities.

Before the 1883 season began, a "harmony conference" was organized in New York City among representatives of the National League, the American Association, and the Northwestern League, a minor league that operated in Michigan, Ohio, and Illinois. A. G. Mills, Hulbert's successor as National League president, represented the N.L., Elias Mather was the spokesman for the Northwestern League, and Denny McKnight presided for the A.A. A tripartite National Agreement was signed to honor the contracts of each of the leagues. The Agreement's main points were mutual recognition of reserved players and the setting up of exclusive territorial rights. Mills also announced that the National League recognized the American Association as having major league status, while the Northwestern League was to be endowed with the rank of a high minor league.

The National League's granting of major league status to the American Association also has a poignant postscript that enables purists to maintain that the first blacks in major league baseball were the Walker brothers of Toledo, not Jackie Robinson, who broke the color line in the national pastime on April 15, 1947. For in 1884 Moses and Welday Walker were members of the American Association Toledo Mudhens.

Moses Fleetwood Walker played in 42 games—41 as a catcher—for Toledo. His brother Welday managed to play in 5 games. Their time with Toledo was marked by many incidents of raw prejudice. Their manager, C. H. Morton, received letters that threatened the life of the brothers. In Louisville, Fleetwood was forced to sit in the stands while his Mudhen team played baseball.

The most outspoken racist of the time was the multitalented Cap Anson, player-manager of Chicago. On July 20, 1884, his White Stockings agreed to play against the Mudhens only after Toledo gave in to demands that Fleetwood Walker be kept off the field.

That 1884 season the International League passed a resolution opposing its teams' participating in any games against squads with black players. The edict was aimed at Buffalo, which had a black second baseman, Frank Grant, and Newark, which had a black pitcher, George Stovey.

Three years later Stovey had the opportunity to break the color line in the National League, but Cap Anson, who openly admitted he had a "dislike for negroes," barred Stovey from competing. No one had the courage to go up against the popular Anson, and major league baseball continued to remain off limits to blacks.

The antiblack feeling in baseball clearly underscored the prejudice of that era in the United States. Blacks were deemed socially inferior, and racists were fond of trotting out the phrase "chocolate-colored coons" to describe black baseball players.

Even players suspected of being black were taunted and run out of organized baseball. In the 1880s Lou Nava was forced out, and in the 1890s George Treadway received the same cruel treatment.

40

No proof existed that either man was black—only a suspicion based on their appearance.

Racist policies deprived fine athletes of the opportunity to make a living in major league baseball. With the color line drawn tight, many blacks had no choice but to play on their own teams in their own league. There was a Negro National League, and the Cuban Giants were one of the strong teams of that era. However even athletes on black teams were made to suffer all types of indignities, including being barred from many hotels and having to resort to sleeping on park benches. As the nineteenth century ended, the average major league white player earned about $2,000 a season, while the top black players made less than $500 for a season.

More organizational strife swirled around professional baseball late in 1883 when the Union Association came into being. The new league claimed that the reserve clause was a form of slavery and began to solicit players from the National League and the American Association. However, the new group's greatest success was in obtaining players from the weak Northwestern League. A blacklist was created by organized baseball to counter the Union Association. Under its provisions, in theory any player who jumped to the new league would be banned from baseball for life. The Union Association had a total of thirty-four teams. Eight cities had two competing Union Association teams, Philadelphia had three.

This unwieldy structure of too many teams in

addition to the power of the existing leagues proved too much of a handicap for the Union Association. It collapsed after the 1884 season, with total losses of almost $250,000. Union Association President Henry V. Lucas, a young St. Louis millionaire, whose team played in the "Palace Park of America," which seated 10,000, had romped to the 1884 pennant. Lucas was allowed to enter the National League with his St. Louis team, to the consternation of American Association leaders, especially St. Louis Browns owner Chris Von der Ahe, who now had a franchise vying directly with his for hometown support. However, Von der Ahe breathed easier when he was told that Lucas's Maroons would not be allowed to charge twenty-five cents for admission, play Sunday ball, or sell beer at the ball park. Lucas's Union Association supporters felt betrayed, but they moved on to other projects, like forming the Western League early in 1885—the organization out of which the American League would come.

In 1885 owners overreached themselves by imposing a contract ceiling of $2,000 per player. That sparked the creation of the first major union of players—the Brotherhood of Professional Base Ball Players. The goals of that organization were to do away with the salary ceiling, modify the reserve clause, and make conditions more palatable for players. The preamble of the organization's constitution promised: "To protect and benefit ourselves collectively and individually. To promote a high standard of professional conduct. To foster and encourage the interests of . . . base ball."

The "reserve clause" was the most restrictive and controlling measure ever put into effect by the owners. In 1879 the owners had engaged in a secret pact to "reserve as property" their five best players. These athletes were not permitted to move to any other team. By 1883 eleven players per team became reserved, and four years later the entire fourteen-man squad of each National League roster was.

William A. Hulbert had argued the merits of the reserve clause thusly: the National League being "a business coalition . . . a perfectly just and proper stroke of business."

Players had no reason to view the reserve clause as just or even proper, but the system was a lifesaver for the owners. It gave them total power to terminate contracts and ban players from the previous practice of annual bargaining with other teams. With the reserve clause as a legal tool, owners were able to trade, sell, or drop a player. The athlete who balked at these conditions had just two alternatives: either try and tolerate them or give up his baseball career.

Within a year of its creation, the Brotherhood boasted a membership of 107 members. John Montgomery Ward was the leader of the group. In 1879 Ward, as a pitcher for Providence, had posted a 44–18 record. Later he became a switch-hitting star infielder for the New York Giants. A handsome, monied sophisticate, Ward was married to a beautiful actress. With all these things going for him, Ward could have easily walked away from bitter battles with owners and the vexing responsibilities of leader-

43

ship of the Brotherhood, but he persisted out of a deep-felt sense of principle.

The owners dug in for the battle. They bribed newspaper editors to slant stories in their favor and to discredit the Brotherhood players, whom they called "hot-headed anarchists" and worse. Albert Spalding headed a "war committee" which threatened some athletes and bribed others to put down the player rebellion. Calumny, vulgarity—all were heaped on the Brotherhood, but Ward and his supporters persisted in their battle for reform, and in some states even won court cases against the reserve clause. However, these decisions were never able to be enforced.

When the 1888 season came to an end, National League club owners escalated their attempts at control. They adopted a classification plan—a kind of rating system for players based on their skills. The salary range was from $2,500 for Class A players down to $1,500 for Class E players. The action of the owners angered players, who at first threatened to strike. Then they backed away and appointed an arbitration committee, attempting to convince the owners to do away with the classification system. Confrontation led to threats, and threats led to hard-line positions on both sides.

All the fighting came to a head on November 4, 1889, when the Players National League of Baseball Clubs was formed to begin play in the 1890 season, with franchises slated for Boston, Brooklyn, Buffalo, Chicago, Cleveland, New York, Philadelphia, and Pittsburgh. Approximately 80 percent of the National

44

League players went over to the new league, including the entire Washington team.

Adrian "Cap" Anson of the Chicago White Stockings and Philadelphia manager Harry Wright were two of the National League legends who refused to go to the new league. However, other big names did jump.

Albert G. Spalding was authorized by the National League to "go after big game." Spalding chose as his target Mike Kelly, "the King," then at the zenith of his career. The lively ballplayer was offered $10,000 by Spalding and a three-year contract. Spalding also gave Kelly a blank check and told him to fill in the amount himself. The following exchange was reported in newspapers of the time.

"What does this mean?" Kelly asked Spalding. "Does it mean that I'm to join the league? Quit the Brotherhood? Go back on the boys?"

"That's just what it means," responded Spalding. "It means that you go to Boston tonight."

"I must have time to think about this," said Kelly.

"There is mighty little time," Spalding pressed him. "If you don't want the money, somebody else will get it. When can you let me know?"

"In an hour and a half."

Kelly returned after spending the ninety minutes walking and thinking.

"Have you decided?" Spalding asked.

"Yes. I decided not to accept."

"What?" Spalding was taken by surprise. "You don't want the ten thousand dollars?"

"Aw, I want the ten thousand bad enough," said Kelly, "but I've thought the matter all over, and I can't go back on the boys. And neither would you. I'm with the Brotherhood."

The Brotherhood's league was a primitive and idealistic attempt at cooperative capitalism. All players were given three-year contracts. A senate of sixteen players, two representing each team, was organized. All teams placed $2,500 into a $20,000 prize fund, to be distributed to teams after the season, with the first-place team to receive $7,000. Another key element of the new league was the provision that if any team made a profit of more than $10,000, the additional profit would be divided equally among all the players in the league. It was a grand experiment in owner-and-player-shared profits and management. Unfortunately it failed.

Although the brand of baseball in the Players League was more skillful and more attractive than in the National League, although the new league compiled a higher attendance that 1890 season than the National League, although the established and wealthier National League lost almost twice as much money that disastrous 1890 season as the Players League, the N.L. had the resources to hold on and the Players League did not. Despite furious protests by members of the Brotherhood, key figures in the Players League worked out a settlement with the National League. The upstart league went under, and the older N.L. simply bought up its players and investors. It was a classic case of a big fish eating a little fish.

"Baseball is a business," observed John Montgomery Ward, "not simply a sport." It was a statement that would echo across the decades to come.

"The baseball war of 1890," noted Connie Mack, "threatened to throw both the National League and the Brotherhood League into bankruptcy. The magnates dropped about four million dollars in their desperate attempt to break the Brotherhood; finally, at great cost, they succeeded. Players scrambled back to their old magnates. They had been suspended for life, but they were received with open arms when they came back as prodigal sons. . . . But the Brotherhood had started a new era in baseball. Club owners had awakened to the realization that ballplayers are human and must be given a fair deal or they will rebel."

A booming prosperity in the 1880s enabled baseball to boom at the turnstiles in both the National League and the American Association. The forerunner of the World Series was in place—postseason competition between the two leagues. However, it was a fumbling, bumbling kind of competition that represented the scatter-gun organization and divisiveness of nineteenth-century baseball.

In 1884 the Providence Grays, National League pennant winner—decided on a percentage basis for the first time—and the New York Metropolitans of the American Association staged a best-of-five-game postseason series. Behind phenomenal pitcher Charles "Old Hoss" Radbourn, who pitched the first three

47

games and won all of them, the Grays won the "world championship." Providence now had bragging rights that it had put the upstart American Association in its place.

That series created a precedent for postseason play between National League and American Association pennant winners over the next half-dozen seasons. In 1885 the National League Chicago White Stockings and the St. Louis Browns of the American Association met in postseason competition—$1,000 dollars in prize money slated for the winner. The competition was a cross between a world series and a barnstorming tour as games were played in Chicago, St. Louis, Pittsburgh, and Cincinnati. There was violence in the stands and on the field, disputes with umpires, slanted news coverage in the press. And when all the fighting, fussing, and playing were over, the final results were murky. Some argued that each team had won three games. Others felt that the Browns were the champs three games to two, since the first game was ruled a forfeit. Chicago recognized the forfeit, but the Browns ignored it. The bottom line was that both owners were content to stop the mad on-field activity after six games rather than go on to a decisive seventh contest. The prize money was equally divided between the two teams and so was the anger players on both clubs felt for each other.

Chicago's Cap Anson claimed that he doubted the Browns could finish even as high as fifth place in the National League. An incensed Bobby Caruthers, St. Louis pitcher, waved a roll of bills at Anson. "I'll bet you one thousand dollars," he shouted, "that the Browns can easily beat your nine. And I'll put this money up as a forfeit."

Chicago shortstop Ned Williamson intervened: "We White Stockings," he snapped, "stand ready to cover all bets the Brown Stockings wish to make."

When the 1886 season came to a close it was clear that the White Stockings were the class of the National League and the Browns once again were the premier club in the American Association. Chicago finished the season with a 90–34 record, winning 24 of its last 34 games; the Browns posted a 93–46 record, winding up their regular season a dozen games in front of second-place Pittsburgh.

The star of St. Louis was Bobby Caruthers, just five feet seven and 138 pounds, dubbed Mighty Mite. He won 30 of his 44 pitching decisions, and also found time to play the outfield and bat .342. Caruthers had a 218–99 record through nine seasons to 1892.

Charles Comiskey was the playing manager of the Browns. Master of the taunt and the tease, he took up a position as close to home plate as possible and unleashed lengthy diatribes and short shots of vulgarity at the opposition, especially catchers.

The larger than life hero of the White Stockings was Michael "King" Kelly, who batted a National League–leading .388 in 1886 and, according to newspaper reports, "could get the nomination for mayor of Chicago on any ticket without making any effort."

The championship series between the two veteran teams called for seven games in seven days—

three in Chicago, three in St. Louis, and the seventh game, if necessary, at a neutral site: Cincinnati. The compactly scheduled competition was necessary due to previous commitments by the Browns, who had arranged to play a best-of-nine series commencing October 14 against their National League counterparts, the St. Louis Maroons.

The Browns went to work on their rigorous postseason schedule, winning four straight from the Maroons, then interrupting that series to begin their series against the White Stockings.

The first four games between the Browns and White Stockings were split; lots of high scoring took place, as well as an experiment in umpiring. The first and third games were officiated by one arbiter. The second and fourth games saw each club appoint an umpire of its choice. These umps were backed up by a referee, "Honest" John Kelly, who was on the scene to straighten out any disagreements between the umpires.

The fourth game was a controversial affair. Second baseman Fred Pfeffer of Chicago allowed a one-out, bases-loaded pop-up to drop in the sixth inning. (This was a normal attempt to initiate a double play in those days before the creation of the infield fly rule.) However, Pfeffer not only failed to start a double play, he manhandled the baseball, opening things up for the underdog Browns to come away with an 8–5 triumph.

Fans and bettors were furious, claiming that the championship series was a hippodrome, a fix, that the White Stockings were allowing the series to extend to make for larger gate receipts in the winner-take-all competition. Cap Anson was furious at the charges. "These games are for blood," he shot back at the allegations of hippodroming. "These games are for the world championship."

The fifth game of the series saw the Browns rout the White Stockings, 10–3, in a game that was stopped after seven innings because of darkness. Al Spalding had to use shortstop Ned Williamson as a starting pitcher and outfielder Jimmy Ryan as a relief pitcher in that contest because of a suddenly sore-armed and exhausted pitching staff.

Sportsman's Park in St. Louis before a crowd of 10,000 was the site of the sixth game. The Browns wore white baseball suits with brown trim of imported English cricket flannel. The White Stockings came to the St. Louis park in horse-drawn carriages, the players decked out in royal blue uniforms, white caps, and long white socks. "It was clear to see," the *Sporting News* reported, "that [both teams] had come out for blood."

After seven innings, the White Stockings led 3–0. One of the runs scored on a fourth-inning long fly ball off the bat of Pfeffer into the right field seats. The ball was still considered in play by the rules of the competition, but the frantic Browns' outfielder was not able to retrieve it in time to retire Pfeffer.

In the eighth inning the Browns scored three runs to tie the score. Two runs came in on Arlie Latham's triple. The player, whose nickname was

"The Freshest Man in the World," had yelled to the crowd as he came to bat: "Don't get nervous, folks, I'll tie it up."

In the St. Louis tenth, outfielder Curt Welch leaned his shoulder into a pitch to get hit by the ball and started to first base. Chicago catcher King Kelly protested. Welch was forced to bat over. He singled, and with one out was on third base. White Stocking pitching ace John Clarkson watched as Welch danced up and down the baseline. Then Clarkson quick-pitched the batter and the ball sailed over catcher Kelly's head. Welch slid home with the winning run. The Browns had defeated the White Stockings, and Welch's run became known, hyperbolically, as the $15,000 slide.

The next day the Browns defeated the Maroons in the climactic but also anticlimactic game of their local championship competition. King Kelly made a presentation to the Browns in the fifth inning of that game against the Maroons. "They have earned it," said a reportedly sober Kelly. "They have beaten our club fairly. We hope to meet them again in the future."

Chris Von der Ahe, St. Louis owner, wanted to play the scheduled seventh game of the World Championship as an exhibition game in Cincinnati. However, Albert Spalding would have no more of the Browns. "We know when we've had enough," he telegraphed Von der Ahe. The teams operated under a winner-take-all formula which awarded the Browns $13,000 for the series. The paunchy Von der Ahe graciously gave each of his players $580 and pocketed the rest. The St. Louis owner had the satisfaction of his team's having defeated the heavily favored Chicago White Stockings of the National League as well as the pride of driving around his city for months in a carriage with horses draped with blankets adorned with the inscription ST. LOUIS BROWNS, CHAMPIONS OF THE WORLD.

In 1887 Detroit challenged St. Louis of the American Association to a 15-game series staged in ten different cities. Total attendance for the 15 games was only 51,455 and total gate receipts were even less. Fans and players were just worn out from all the rigors of a 15-game series. For the record, the Detroit National League team won 10 of the 15 games they played against the Browns.

In 1888 the postseason competition was mercifully reduced to 10 games. The St. Louis Browns took the field against the New York Nationals. St. Louis owner Chris Von der Ahe did it up big. He hired a special train for his players and guests. Viewing the baseball doings as one lavish party, the St. Louis beer baron bought a suit of clothes for each of his athletes and special guests. Celebrating with huge grogs of beer and other spirits made the St. Louis players feel no pain, but it did little for their athletic ability, and many wondered how St. Louis was able to win even four of the ten games played. The total affair cost Von der Ahe almost $50,000, but he was philosophical about it all, claiming the entire thing "was lots of fun and a good investment."

Brooklyn of the American Association and the New York Nationals went head to head in more sedate postseason play in 1889, as the New Yorkers won, 6 games to 3. In 1890, Louisville players claimed they were "tuckered out" and quit postseason play against the Brooklyn Nationals when their series was tied up at three all.

Although inconsistency of play, apathy, and lunacy of logistics reduced attendance in those nineteenth-century postseason encounters, they did plant the seeds for the World Series of the future. It was also the first time in the history of baseball that most teams operated in the black. Player salaries escalated accordingly as the two leagues waged an all-out battle for talent.

And although the National Agreement was in place, it was often ignored. In the American Association, Brooklyn and St. Louis were perennial battlers for the pennant and control of the league's management. In 1890 a puppet of the St. Louis Browns was made president of the American Association. Brooklyn and Cincinnati abandoned the Association and jumped to the National League, which ignored the principles of the National Agreement and readied itself for all-out battle versus the A.A. That was also the year that the Players League came into being. Competing against two leagues was too much for the Association. In 1890 the Players League drew 980,888. The National League attendance was 813,678, while the Association was third with a reported 500,000. Its attendance in decline, some of its players departing for better pay, the Association was reeling. And by

1891, it was through—a footnote to baseball history. Four of its clubs were taken into what became a twelve-team National League, and the remaining four were bought out.

On the playing field there were several historic moments. In 1894, Hugh Duffy of Boston batted an astounding .438. His teammate Bobby Lowe became the first man in history to hit four home runs in one game. A year later Ed Delahanty became the second player to hit four home runs in a game. "Big Ed" was presented with four boxes of chewing gum for his classic clouts. In 1897 "Wee Willie" Keeler hit safely in 44 straight games—a record that would endure for 44 seasons. And that 1897 season, a powerfully formed, bowlegged player made his National League debut. His name was Honus Wagner.

As the century drew toward its close, a myriad of problems, a quest for order, and a struggle for survival characterized the tone and the tempo of baseball. Only Chicago and Boston of the original National League franchises still fielded teams in 1890. Between 1877 and 1890, twenty-three different cities had been represented in the National League—a circuit which in that time period never had more than eight teams in one season.

As the final decade wore on, the National League continued to cope with huge debts that it had accumulated in its war with the Brotherhood. Additionally, the absorption of the four teams from the American Association created many burdens in the league's image and attendance. Louisville and St. Louis were the weak sisters of the National League—they drew very poorly. And the Giants of New York, a flagship franchise, were no longer competitive on the field, further weakening the strength of the National League.

Riotous behavior by players, a conspicuous use of indecent and obscene language, umpire baiting—all of these further tarnished the image of an unwieldy and obtuse twelve-team National League throughout the 1890s.

As the nineteenth century came to a close, political bickering among owners, a salary ceiling of $2,400 that infuriated players, lively competition from other entertainment sources, inability to consummate plans to create two six-team divisions—all were part of the thick web of problems afflicting the National League scene.

And so was the franchise from Cleveland, a team that painfully revealed the league's imbalance. The players wore white and dark blue uniforms, and a club executive assessing their not too robust shape remarked: "They look skinny and spindly, just like spiders. Might as well call them Spiders and be done with it."

That pathetic aggregation won 20 games and lost 134 that 1899 season, for a winning percentage of .130, and finished dead, dead last—84 games behind pennant-winning Brooklyn. Cleveland's sorry pitching staff had a 30-game loser, a 22-game loser, and two hurlers who suffered 35 defeats between them. The Spiders were last in runs scored, doubles, triples, home runs, batting average, slugging percent-age, stolen bases. Only once that 1899 season did they win 2 games in a row, and on six occasions they had losing streaks of 11 or more games.

That year of 1899 was the final season of the Cleveland Spiders. The following winter the National League went back to eight teams; Cleveland, Washington, Louisville, and Baltimore were cut out.

In 1900 the reorganized eight-team National League consisted of Boston, Brooklyn, Cincinnati, New York, Philadelphia, Pittsburgh, and St. Louis. It was a pattern that would remain intact until 1953—those eight teams of the National League whose names virtually every schoolboy would be able to recite by heart.

In 1893 Byron Bancroft Johnson, known as Ban, then president of the Western League—the strongest and most solvent of the minor leagues—began to dream his dream of a second major league. With his league's franchises located in the Midwest, with his lieutenant Charles Comiskey heading the successful St. Paul club, the former sportswriter Johnson believed that he could succeed where others had failed in achieving parity with the National League. The Western League differed sharply in ambience from the old second major league: no liquor was allowed in the ball parks, player decorum was monitored, umpires were sup-ported, and attendance by women was encouraged.

In 1900 Ban Johnson renamed his league the American League and asked the National League to classify his new circuit as a major league. His request was met with scorn and ridicule by the National League moguls; they had been through this sort of thing before.

Johnson explained that his desire for major league status for the American League was motivated by "self-preservation." He also explained that his new league would provide protection for the National League against the actions of other groups who might be unfriendly to the Nationals. Finally, Johnson maintained that ". . . we in the American [League] wish to act wholly in concert with the National and on absolutely friendly terms."

The National League showed its disdain for the new American League and its request for major league status by having its secretary, Nick Young, send a letter to Johnson asking the new league to remit its fees—a traditional bit of homage for minor leagues. Johnson sent a letter but no fees back to Young. In his letter Johnson explained that no fees were being paid to the National League because the American League considered itself a viable major league candidate.

"We will become a major league, whether the Nationals wish it or not," said Johnson. He also made it clear that his new league planned to expand into eastern (National) territory in 1901.

When the 1900 season ended, Johnson appointed a "circuit committee" made up of himself, Charles Comiskey, now the Chicago team owner, and Charles Somers, owner of the Cleveland club. The mission of the committee was to survey selected cities in the East "as to their appropriate baseball backgrounds."

Connie Mack secured backing for an American League franchise in Philadelphia. The owner of the 1900 Milwaukee team agreed to support its transfer to Washington. And Wilbert Robinson and John McGraw announced that they would sponsor a team in Baltimore. A Boston group also was eager to finance a team for 1901.

Boston was virtually sacred National League territory, and rather than push too hard, Johnson told National League leaders that he wished to meet with them to discuss all possibilities. The December 1900 National League conference was designated as the place for the meeting. Johnson was kept waiting for hours outside the door of the National League conference. Finally, the Nationals, completing their business, slipped out a side door, ignoring Johnson.

An announcement was made to the press that the National League would operate a new minor league in the Midwest in 1901 and would include Minneapolis and Kansas City as part of the operation. The National League announcement was a dagger pointed directly at the American League.

White with anger, Johnson snarled. "Well, if they want a real war, they can have war."

In 1901 Johnson claimed official major league status for his new league and yet another baseball war was on. The 1901 American League teams were Chicago, Detroit, Milwaukee, and Cleveland in the West; Boston, Baltimore, Washington, and Philadelphia in the East. The lure of money—more money than the $2,400 N.L. salary ceiling—brought some of the brightest stars into the American League: Cy

Young, Joe McGinnity, Napoleon Lajoie, John McGraw, Jimmie Collins, Wee Willie Keeler, Bobby Wallace, Ed Delahanty, Jack Chesbro . . .

The new American League honored contracts but chose to ignore the reserve clause. At least seventy players ultimately moved over to the American League, which drew more than 2,000,000 fans in 1902, to fewer than 1,700,000 for the National League. Finally, after two years of financial losses, the National League owners reluctantly agreed to sue for peace with the American League. The Nationals sought to consolidate both leagues into a twelve-team circuit, but Johnson refused. In the final peace settlement—the National Agreement of 1902—the American League was permitted to retain most of the players who had come over from the National League. The two circuits then agreed to honor each other's reserve rights and contracts. The new agreement also protected the minor leagues: their territorial rights were secured, and they were granted reserve rights for players. And a system was enacted that set up machinery for major league teams to draft players from minor league teams and pay the minor league teams for the contracts of these players.

In essence, peace between the National League and the American League solidified baseball's business foundation, consolidated all the gains of the sport in the nineteenth century, and set the tone for twentieth-century baseball.

Conscious control of the style and the substance of the game were always the primary concerns of the club owners. There was constant tinkering with rules. The owners—who preferred to be called magnates—overreached and overreacted. Bickering, almost for the sake of bickering, it seemed, became a cornerstone of organized baseball. Changes in rules, the disbursement of gate receipts, selection and behavior of umpires, player salaries and behavior, franchise solvency and insolvency—all of these and more, frequently formed the subject matter of acrimonious meetings and encounters among the magnates. The most positive changes in the game were in the rules enacted that moved baseball closer in look and tone to the twentieth century.

Baseball played in 1876 bore some resemblance to the game of today, but its style was very different. The baseball weighed not less than 5 ounces and no more than 5½ ounces. Its circumference was no less than 9 inches nor more than 9½ inches. Those dimensions of the baseball have remained the same throughout the history of the national pastime, but other features of the game have undergone dramatic changes.

In 1876 the pitcher (still referred to in some circles as a "bowler") stood 45 feet away from a maskless catcher and threw underhand to the plate. The more successful pitchers depended a great deal on their ability to vary the velocity of their pitches. The catcher stood a few feet behind the batter and worked hard at catching the ball on its first bounce.

Batters had the privilege of directing hurlers to throw the ball "high" or "low." There was no formal strike zone, and nine balls constituted a walk. An "unfair" ball delivered by the hurler was a pitch not to the batter's liking. Once a batter had two strikes and allowed a third "good pitch" to go by a warning was issued by the umpire. If the pitcher delivered a fourth "good pitch," and it was not swung at, the batter was retired on a "called strikeout." Batters were charged with a time at bat if they walked. The more successful hitters made an art of slamming the pitched ball through the infield, and hard grounders became staples of batting success. Gloves for fielders would not come until later.

The look of the playing field was a major concern of the rules makers in 1877. Home plate was moved from its position just back of the edge of the diamond to a spot exactly within the diamond or square—the location it occupies today. Rules were also instituted that mandated a 15-inch-square canvas-covered base as standard.

In 1879, pitchers enjoyed their final season of being allowed to serve up nine balls before a batter was awarded first base on a walk. By 1882, seven balls meant a walk. And in 1889, the present regulation of four balls constituting a walk came into being and became the standard for professional baseball. That season of 1879, the rule that declared a runner out if he was hit by a batted ball was adopted. It was a much needed regulation, eliminating the practice of base runners' running into a ball to prevent infielders from making a play.

In 1880, hurlers moved five feet farther from the batters when the pitching distance to home plate was changed from 45 feet to 50 feet. That same year the National League owners announced that players could be barred "from play and from pay" for "insubordination or misconduct of any kind." Albert Spalding in 1882 made his Chicago players sign a pledge that they would totally abstain from the consumption of whiskey, wine, and beer. Spalding brooked no nonsense. Enforcement of the pledge came in the form of a private detective who was hired to snoop on players.

All types of unusual, some would say outlandish, uniforms existed prior to 1882. That season the National League ruled that teams would no longer be allowed free choice in baseball fashion. Clubs were also restricted to the use of designated colors: Boston, red; Cleveland, navy blue; Chicago, white; Providence, light blue; Buffalo, gray; Troy, green; Detroit, old gold; Worcester, brown. By 1883, regulations for uniforms were rescinded and applied only to the color of stockings.

Change, new beginnings, constantly characterized the baseball climate. Pitchers were emancipated in 1884 when all restrictions on their windups were removed. Now hurlers were free to use any type of motion they desired just as long as they faced the batter at the moment of their windup. In 1885, batters were permitted to use bats with one flat side—and paddle at the ball. Pitchers that year were credited with an assist on a batter's strike-out.

Several of the changes in rules and innovations developed by teams attempted to speed up the game and to cut down on unruly behavior. By the mid-1880s, fixed coaching lines were in place. In theory coaches were now restricted to plying their trade from a designated area and not running up and down in a helter-skelter manner, venting their opinions. The fixed coaching lines helped a bit, but many of the coaches still strayed about at will.

Some of the playing fields were enclosed by four-foot wooden fences to keep overly exuberant fans in their place and off the field of play. These barriers were effective and kept mobs at bay.

In 1886, the game was speeded up a bit more when the five-minute "lost ball" rule was dropped. Umpires were now allowed to replace a lost ball instantaneously rather than follow the previous practice of allowing players five minutes to forage for a lost ball before a new ball was put into play.

The year 1886 witnessed some intriguing new rules. The captain of the home team was allowed to decide which team batted first. The pitcher's box was enlarged from 6 × 4 feet to 7 × 4 feet. And the troublesome rule that credited a runner with a stolen base for each base he advanced on another player's hit came into being. Not until 1898 was the present stolen base rule put into effect.

Experimentation and also some lasting changes marked the 1887 season. For that year only, four strikes were allowed a batter—the initial called third strike did not count—and walks were counted in the batting average of a player as hits. A batter was also allowed to take first base when struck by a pitch—a rule that has lasted until the present day. Pitchers in

1887 were banned for all time from taking a run and a jump before delivering the ball. And batters lost for all time their privilege of demanding a "high" or a "low" pitch. From 1887 on they had had to go for what was served up.

Not all the rules promulgated, however, added to the forward movement of the game. The 1887 rules counting a walk as a hit and allowing batters four strikes put the hitters on parade. A dozen of them batted over .400 that 1894 season.

Recomputation today of those averages, taking away the "walk hits," leaves only three hitters with averages over .400. Harry Stovey, a .402 batter, recomputed, drops to .286. Tip O'Neill of the American Association St. Louis Browns batted a glittering .492 and was the league leader in runs, doubles, triples, and homers. Tip didn't walk a lot and his recomputed batting average is still a lofty .442.

In 1888 the three strike rule was restored and a walk was no longer credited in a player's batting average as a hit or a time at bat. Thus, the game moved even closer to the rules of today. However, a revisionist step also was enacted that year crediting a batter with a hit when his batted ball hit a base runner. That 1888 season also saw the enactment of a rule that a ball hit over the fence in fair territory was a ground-rule double and not a home run if the fence was less than 210 feet from home plate.

Balls and strikes in 1889 moved closer to the standard pattern that has persisted to this day when a rule mandated that four balls equal a walk. Other changes that year included no error charged to the catcher on a passed ball, no error assigned to a pitcher for a walk, wild pitch, balk, or hit batter. The sacrifice bunt was also recognized, but the batter executing it was charged with a time at bat.

Prior to 1891, substitutions were allowed in a game only when a player was injured or when permission was granted by the opposing team. That 1891 season the lasting pattern for substitution came into being: substitution was now allowed at any time during a game.

In 1893 a misreading of a diagram set the pitching distance from the mound—where a rubber slab 12 inches long and 4 inches wide was now mandatory—to home plate at 60 feet 6 inches. Actually, the rules makers had changed the distance from 50 feet to 60 feet, but the surveyor read 60 feet as 60' 6". And that is how the distance has remained to this time. Another rule mandated that all bats be completely round. That 1893 season the rule came into being that a sacrifice would not be counted as a time at bat for a hitter.

From 1894 to the end of the century still more rule refinements made the game of baseball more closely approximate in style and substance what it is today. Some of the major changes in rules in those years included: Attempted bunts that went foul were ruled strikes. The infield fly rule was introduced. A foul tip was a strike. The maximum diameter of a bat was increased from 2½ inches to 2¾ inches. Errors were not charged to infielders attempting to complete a double play unless throws were so errant that runners were able to gain an extra base, and catchers were not charged with errors when attempting to prevent a stolen base unless they threw so wildly that runners were able to gain an additional base. The balk rule was adopted. Batters were allowed to run past first base without being tagged out after returning to the bag. The present day five-sided plate was introduced.

As the twentieth century began, the pitcher threw overhand from the mound to the batter, who swung at a ball not nearly as lively as the one used today. Batters worked on the art and science of hitting, while base runners worked on their maneuvers on the bases. Catchers were stationed immediately behind home plate with regalia including mask, chest protector, and heavy mitt. The days of the gloveless wonders were all but gone; most fielders sported mitts of some type—skimpy and frail as they were compared to those in use today. Newspapers of the time covered the daily doings of baseball teams and their stars, who were rapidly becoming America's folk heroes. Journalistic baseball jargon, press partiality to the home team, and obsession by reporters with statistics were all part of the scene.

In the America of 1900, 31 million people lived in cities and 46 million dwelled in rural areas. In the America of 1900 the *New York Times* noted: ". . . Rowdyism by the players on the field, syndicalism among the club owners, poor umpiring and talk of rival organizations . . . are the principal causes for baseball's decline."

The game nevertheless had survived through the

nineteenth century, through its crossroads time, through primitive baseball, to move into the new century. Baseball had evolved into a blend of hitting and pitching, defense and offense. It had changed radically from the way it was in its early years as a result of all the tinkerings, refinements, and rules changes. Nuance and geometry were mixed and matched, and mixed and matched some more, making baseball more appealing to fans, more balanced for the players, more a game that would stake its claim as America's premier sport of the twentieth century, the national pastime.

III
Cast of Characters:
A Sampler

They peer out of faded photographs, those nineteenth-century baseballers. Some have mustaches and others have beards and still others have the clean-shaven faces of innocents playing ball in a more innocent time. They were the pioneers of a sport, the trailblazers.

By the end of the nineteenth century, baseball was a sport that provided a step up, a glamorous career opportunity, for youth coming out of lower socioeconomic origins. Few of them ever attended college and few of them ever moved into professional work in their life after baseball. Their playing careers were generally short and then they moved into blue-collar jobs.

Many of the players came from big cities, especially the booming northeastern metropolitan areas. In 1897, for example, just 3 out of 168 National League players came from as far south as Virginia. Only 7 players came from the West, while more than a third of the athletes were born in Pennsylvania or Massachusetts.

All of them were white (with a couple of brief exceptions), and the bulk of the players were from German or Irish backgrounds. Fun-loving, spree-oriented, generous spenders, the nineteenth-century baseball players were a lively assortment of athletes. They brought a verve, a daring, a love to the game that enabled the sport to surmount obstacles and to prevail.

DAN BROUTHERS

The man who was the "Babe Ruth of his day," Dan Brouthers personified power hitting. His 1886 clout out of Washington's Capitol Park was the storied tape measure shot of its time. That same year Brouthers smashed a home run out of the ball park in Boston that banged into Sullivan's Tower, scattering fans who up to that point thought they had a safe, free, and unobstructed view of the game.

The first player to win back-to-back batting titles (1882 and 1883), Brouthers had a chance at three in a row in 1884, but a sprained ankle kept him from recording that feat.

The powerfully built six footer batted .300 or more fourteen times, while compiling a lifetime batting average of .343. At the advanced baseball age of forty-eight, Dennis "Dan" Brouthers was still plying his trade in the high minor leagues.

JESSE BURKETT

A member of the Cleveland Spiders through most of the 1890s, Burkett played major league baseball in two different centuries. He shares the distinction along with Rogers Hornsby of being the only player in baseball history to bat .400 or better three times. A batting champion in 1895 (.423) and 1896 (.410), Burkett also batted .402 in 1899, but lost his chance for another batting crown that season because Philadelphia's Ed Delahanty batted .408. Burkett was one of baseball's most exceptional bunters and batted leadoff through most of his career.

Only five feet eight inches and 155 pounds and all short fuse, Burkett was known as the Crab, a nickname his not too genial personality earned for him. Some observers noted that Burkett, an insulter of opposing players, an inciter of fans, was a one-man riot. "Other players are bigger and huskier," the outspoken Burkett explained. "I have to make up for the difference somehow."

FRED CLARKE

Born on October 3, 1872, in Winterset, Iowa, Fred Clifford Clarke joined Louisville in the National League in 1894. He rapped out five hits—the first of his 2,703 lifetime hits—in five at bats in his major league debut. "Those pitchers had a hell of a time knocking the bat out of my hand," he remembered happily.

In mid-season of 1897, Clarke, then a twenty-four-year-old established star, was appointed player-manager of the Louisville team by owner Barney Dreyfuss. Though the hustling Clarke batted .406 that season—he would have won the batting title except for the fact that Wee Willie Keeler hit .432—Clarke's teammates were not up to his high standards. The Colonels finished as usual in the lower depths of the National League standings. During the next two seasons, Clarke managed to push the Colonels to ninth-place finishes in a twelve-team league.

In 1900, when the National League constricted to eight teams, Louisville was put out of business. Dreyfuss acquired a half interest in the newly formed Pittsburgh team—a collection of the best of the leftovers of other clubs. In the new century Clarke's star rose. With the Pittsburgh Pirates, Clarke became the manager of the first dominant team of the twentieth century.

JOHN CLARKSON

Adrian "Cap" Anson had this to say of John Clarkson after his death in 1909: "Clarkson was one of the greatest pitchers of all time, certainly the best Chicago ever had. Many regard him as the greatest, but not many know of his peculiar temperament and the amount of encouragement needed to keep him going. Scold him, find fault with him, and he could not pitch at all. Praise him, and he was unbeatable. In knowing what kind of a ball a batter could not hit and his ability to serve up that kind of ball, I don't think I have ever seen the equal of Clarkson."

John Gibson Clarkson was a force, powering Chicago to three straight pennants, winning 53 games in 1885, 35 in 1886, and 38 in 1887. Then he was sold to Boston for the fabled figure (for those days) of $10,000.

A terrific fastball accounted for Clarkson's early success, and when he lost some of his speed he added a drop curveball and a change of pace to his bag of tricks. Always adjusting, Clarkson further refined his skills by honing his control to the point where he became a master of any pitching situation.

With all he had going for him Clarkson had too brief a major league career. It was cut short by his witnessing a horrible train accident involving his catcher and buddy, Charley Bennett. The accident resulted in Bennett's losing parts of both legs and Clarkson becoming somewhat unbalanced. He pitched for just one season after that—1894 for Cleveland.

JIMMIE COLLINS

Hall of Famer Jimmie Collins held down third base in the greatest infield in nineteenth-century baseball. His mates at Boston included Fred Tenney at first base, Bobby Lowe at second, and Herman Long at shortstop. It was Collins who totally revolutionized the way third basemen played their position. He was the first third baseman to play off the base, the first to play shallow and charge the ball, use his quick

73

reflexes to spear the ball barehanded and fire it to first base.

Collins even made the skeptical Baltimore Orioles into believers. In one memorable game, John McGraw bunted. Collins charged, speared, and fired the ball to first base. McGraw was retired. Wee Willie Keeler bunted. Collins repeated his act. Keeler was retired. Four Orioles in succession attempted to bunt their way on. Four Orioles in a row were retired by Collins. They got the message and ceased bunting on him.

For five seasons with Boston, James Joseph Collins, a native of Buffalo, New York, averaged 300 or more assists a year. His lifetime batting average was .294, but it was the glove of Collins that was the biggest argument for his admission to baseball's Hall of Fame and his reputation as one of the top players in nineteenth-century baseball.

ROGER CONNOR

A powerfully built Irishman, Roger Connor began his playing career with Troy in the National League in 1880. He went on to become one of the first great power hitters in baseball, recording 132 home runs from 1880 to 1897. He also ranks among the all-time career leaders in triples, with 227.

Connor's time spent as a slugging first baseman for the New York Giants enhanced his reputation as "Dear Old Rog." One of his most memorable home runs was hit out of the old Polo Grounds at 110th

74

Street and Fifth Avenue in New York City. The ball made its way over the right field fence and finally came to rest on 112th Street. Fans gave Connor a $500 gold watch as a trophy to commemorate the event.

Connor's most prolific day at the plate took place on June 1, 1895. He was then playing for the St. Louis Browns against his old team, the New York Giants. He went six for six.

CANDY CUMMINGS

As a young man strolling the beaches in Brooklyn in 1865, Arthur Cummings noticed that clam shells tossed underhand would curve to the right. In boarding school, Cummings played around with a baseball, and with a horizontal whip of the wrist was able to make the ball rise and drop. Thus was the curveball born. Actually what Cummings did was to snap his wrist and the second finger of his right hand when releasing the ball, making it curve.

His first highly publicized exhibition of what a curveball could do took place in 1867 when he was pressed into service as a member of the Excelsiors of Brooklyn, then playing against the Harvards of Cambridge. The curveball that Cummings threw, in the words of one Harvard player, "came at us and then went away from us."

The curveball became widely imitated and the pitcher's best friend after others saw what Candy Cummings was able to accomplish with it. From 1868 to 1872 Cummings pitched for the Stars of Brooklyn, a group that called itself the "championship team of the United States and Canada." He then plied his trade with the Mutuals and other teams. By 1877, the 120-pound Cummings was through—his touch was gone. The legacy of Candy Cummings was the curveball— the pitch that changed the game and enabled its inventor to become a member of baseball's Hall of Fame.

ED DELAHANTY

One of five Irish brothers who excited the world of baseball around the turn of the century, Edward James Delahanty was the biggest and the best athlete of the quintet.

On a July afternoon in 1896 he became the second player in history to stroke four home runs in a game. In a sixteen-year major league career, the Hall of Famer recorded 2,597 hits and a lifetime batting average of .346. Delahanty as a member of the Philadelphia Phillies batted .408 to lead the National League in hitting in 1899. Three years later he led the American League in hitting.

Just one of eight players to bat .400 or better twice, Delahanty notched a .400 average in 1894. However that fabled figure was good enough only for fourth place in the batting race behind Hugh Duffy, Tuck Turner, and Sam Thompson. Turner and Thompson were teammates of Big Ed on a Philadelphia team that collectively batted .349 for the season.

Delahanty did bat a .408 in 1899, which was more than good enough for him to win the batting title that year.

HUGH DUFFY

Hugh Duffy began his major league playing career with Chicago in 1888 in the National League. He finished it in 1908 as a member of Providence in the Eastern League. Duffy's most sublime season was 1894; playing for the Boston Beaneaters, he batted .438—the highest season batting average in major league baseball history.

In 124 games, Duffy managed 236 hits. In only 17 games did he fail to hit safely. Twice he stroked 5 hits in a game, and twelve times he rapped out 4 hits.

"No one thought that much of averages in those days," Duffy recalled with a smile. "I didn't realize I had hit that much until the official averages were published four months later."

As a "reward" for his accomplishment, Duffy's salary was raised $12.50 a week, making his annual take $2,750. With the added moneys, however, went added responsibilities. Duffy was made team captain and charged with ensuring that all bats and balls were returned to the clubhouse after games.

When Duffy began his career with the White Stockings, manager Cap Anson was not too impressed with the five-foot-seven outfielder. "Where's the rest of you?" asked the tough Anson. "That's all there is," was Duffy's reply. It was not enough for Anson.

Duffy played just two seasons for Chicago—and Anson never quite got over having given up on the sweet-swinging future Hall of Famer.

BUCK EWING

Acknowledged as the first catcher to crouch behind the plate, William "Buck" Ewing was the dominant backstop of nineteenth-century baseball. John B. Foster, editor of the *Spalding Baseball Guide*, observed of the man who was the star catcher for the New York National League team of the 1880s:

"Buck could throw from any position. It was not by accident that he could throw fearlessly and unswervingly when he squatted down behind the batter, but he chose to throw that way, because he knew he could and did catch runners with the same easy skill that he would have caught them if he were standing."

The sharp snap of the forearm Ewing utilized to launch the ball to his fielders enabled them to catch base runners off guard. On the bases, Ewing turned the tables, recording impressive stolen base totals for himself. He didn't really have much speed, but studied opposing pitchers and knew when to make his move. Once he stole second and third base and shouted: "Now I'm stealing home." He did what he claimed he would. And that play was memorialized on a lithograph that was treasured by New York City sports fans of the time.

Ewing batted .303 and stole 336 bases in an

eighteen-year career that ended in 1897. He was admitted to baseball's Hall of Fame in 1939.

PUD GALVIN

In the all-time top ten in wins, losses, complete games, games started, and shutouts, Pud Galvin was the Walter Johnson of his time—1879 to 1892.

Known as Gentle Jeems, and the Little Steam Engine, the five-foot-eight-inch 190-pound right-hander was paid this tribute by Buck Ewing:

"If I had Galvin to catch, no one would ever steal a base on me. That fellow keeps 'em glued to the bases and also has the best control of any pitcher in the league."

Pure power and control made Galvin a master practitioner of pitching excellence. He won 46 games, working the staggering total of 656 innings in 1883. In 1884 he again won 46 games. His 5,959 lifetime innings pitched is more than any other hurler in baseball history except for Cy Young.

Galvin's greatest years were with Buffalo, where during a six-day period in 1884 he hurled a one-hitter, then a three-hitter, and then a third game of eleven innings of shutout ball.

Ironically, with all of his storied pitching accomplishments, it was not until sixty-three years after his death that James Francis Galvin was finally admitted to baseball's Hall of Fame.

CLARK GRIFFITH

Born on November 20, 1869, in Stringtown, Missouri, Clark Calvin Griffith is best-known as a manager and an owner, but he was also one of the top pitchers for Cap Anson's Chicago team in the 1890s.

Dubbed the Old Fox because of his thinking approach to pitching, Griffith had many battles with John McGraw. Once the old Baltimore Oriole singled and was on first base taunting Griffith. The umpire suggested that Griffith pick off McGraw, but with the small lead the arrogant Oriole was assuming it was not a feasible tactic.

"Balk him off," the umpire suggested. Griffith followed orders, purposely balking to first base. No balk was called by the umpire. McGraw protested so vociferously that he was thrown out of the game by the umpire. Griffith attempted the same technique with the next batter who reached first base safely. It was to no avail. "Balks work only with McGraw," the ump explained.

Griffith, however, didn't really have to resort to chicanery—his talent was enough to reel off six straight 20-win seasons in the 1890s.

BILLY HAMILTON

Stocky Billy Hamilton played from 1888 to 1901, and in that time stole 912 bases. Three years in a row he stole over a hundred bases. His steals and his slides earned him his nickname, "Sliding Billy." His exploits on the basepaths and a .344 lifetime batting average were more than good enough to get him admitted to baseball's Hall of Fame.

The 1894 season was just one of the zeniths of Hamilton's career. He scored 196 runs in 131 games, batted .399, and also drove catcher Deacon McGuire of Washington crazy in one game by stealing seven bases, tying a record set in 1881 by Chicago's George Gore.

The Newark, New Jersey, native played for Philadelphia and then for Boston, where he was a teammate of the great Hugh Duffy. Hamilton, a former high school sprinter, led the charge for the pennant by the 1897 Beaneaters—scoring 153 runs, batting .344. His career stolen base record stood for decades until Lou Brock of the St. Louis Cardinals came along.

HUGHIE JENNINGS

In 1894 Hugh Ambrose Jennings joined the Baltimore Orioles of John J. McGraw, Wee Willie Keeler, Dan Brouthers, Wilbert Robinson, Joe Kelley—all future Hall of Famers. Jennings profited greatly from being in such an exceptional environment for the honing of baseball skills.

A skillful and speedy base runner, Jennings was also a fine fielding shortstop. Five times he led the National League in fielding. "Hughie Jennings," said

Honus Wagner, "was the first shortstop never to leave his position until the hitter either hit the ball or missed it. He had wonderful reflexes." The legendary Wagner also acknowledged a personal debt to Jennings, claiming that he modeled much of his defensive approach after that of the tough Baltimore Oriole shortstop.

Jennings was both a survivor and an intellect. Three times he came back from skull fractures. His faculties unimpaired from the stresses and ravages of tough National League baseball, he earned a law degree from Cornell and went on to become one of baseball's greatest managers.

TIM KEEFE

The son of Irish immigrants, Tim Keefe was a mainstay of the New York Giants from 1885 to 1889. Keefe was a gentle and soft-spoken man and was given the affectionate nickname "Sir Timothy."

The well-built right-hander ranks in the all-time top ten in wins, complete games, and innings pitched. Keefe possessed a good fast ball and curve, but his change of pace so effectively complemented his other pitches that it was his complete repertoire that made him an outstanding hurler.

His sensitivity was reflected in an 1887 incident. One of his fastballs struck Boston second baseman John Burdock on the temple. And Keefe was so unsettled by what he had done that he suffered a nervous breakdown and missed a few weeks of the season.

After his incredible 1888 season—35 wins, 12 losses, a 1.74 earned run average, and 333 strikeouts— Keefe was signed to a contract of $4,500 a year, making him the highest paid player on the New York Giants.

WEE WILLIE KEELER

On September 30, 1892, William Henry Keeler made his debut at the Polo Grounds as a member of the New York Giants. He singled off Tim Keefe of the Phillies and the first of his 2,926 hits was now in the record books.

Two years later Keeler, the son of a Brooklyn trolley switchman, became a member of the Baltimore Orioles. Only five feet four and 140 pounds, the left-handed hitting Keeler more than made up for his lack of size with fine running speed and deft bat control. He hit the ball where it was pitched or, in his phrase, "hit 'em where they [the fielders] ain't."

Keeler opened the 1897 season with two hits in five at bats against Boston. For two months the small southpaw swinger slapped hit after hit, game after game, from April 22 to June 18—for 44 straight games. His record stood for forty-four years, until Joe DiMaggio snapped it in 1941.

In 1899, Keeler returned to his place of birth and was a member of the Brooklyn team, which won pennants that year and the next. Thus, in his first seven seasons as a regular player, Keeler's teams won five pennants and twice finished second. With him in the lineup, clubs scored a lot of runs. The little man's .345 lifetime batting average ranks him fifth on the all-time list.

JOE KELLEY

Since the Baltimore Orioles were one of the most dominant teams of nineteenth-century baseball, it is no surprise that many of the dominant players performed for the O's. Joe Kelley was not only a dominant player, he was also one of the most unusual.

One of his props was a mirror that he kept in his pocket and from time to time used as he stood out in left field waiting for some action. The mirror was useful for Kelley, enabling him to primp and pamper his ample face more effectively.

Kelley was always active in left field, sometimes burying balls in the tall grass—little decoys at the ready, available for Kelley's employment when the right moment came along.

From 1893 on, Kelley batted over .300 for a dozen straight seasons. One of his greatest campaigns was 1894—he batted .391 and stole 45 bases. And on September 3 of that year, he managed a record nine hits in nine at bats in a doubleheader—three singles and a triple in the first game, four doubles and a single in the second game.

Energetic, attractive, talented, Joseph James Kelley, a native of Cambridge, Massachusetts, was one of the most popular players of his time.

84

Two men fundamental to baseball's beginnings: Alexander Cartwright, Jr. (left), the actual father of the game (here shown, circa 1870, as the fire chief of Honolulu, where he later settled); and Albert Spalding (right), circa 1875, pitcher par excellence and later baseball's premier entrepreneur. Below, in baseball's first action shot, Union troops stand in parade formation at Fort Pulaski, Savannah, Georgia, 1862 or 1863, before a baseball game in progress.

Moses Fleetwood Walker (above), baseball's first black major-league player, in 1884. Both Fleetwood and his brother, Welday, were educated at Oberlin College, Ohio (they are pictured below in Oberlin's first varsity baseball team: Fleetwood, number 6; Welday, number 10), and both played for the Toledo Mudhens—until Adrian "Cap" Anson (right), the legendary player-manager of the Chicago White Stockings in the 1880s and the most powerful racist in the business, demanded that Fleetwood be removed from the field.

Baseball fashions: what the teams of the 1870s wore. Note, above, that the first team to adopt shortened pants was the Cincinnati Red Stockings. John McGraw (right), major force behind three Baltimore Oriole pennants in the 1890s, in warm-up gear. The Chicago White Stockings (below), baseball's first great team and National League champions in 1880, 1881, 1882, and 1885. Clarkson is in front, second from the right; Anson behind, third from the left; King Kelly, behind Carlson.

The Boston South End Grounds (above), which burned down on May 15, 1894. Spectators had been distracted by a fight involving McGraw at third base, then fled to the field for safety as the fire raged. Miraculously no one was hurt, though the fire claimed some 150 homes in the vicinity. The Providence Grays (below), 1884 National League champions and winner of the first post-season competition, winning the best of five games over the New York Metropolitans.

The New York Giants (above), National League champions of 1889. Below, the Young Ladies Baseball Club No. 1, 1890–91. The team traveled from city to city, playing exhibition games against themselves or against men's teams. While there is some question whether all the young ladies were indeed female, the games nonetheless attracted crowds as well as press censure—baseball was not a seemly sport for Victorian young ladies.

John Montgomery Ward, above left, one of baseball's first superstars: pitcher, in-fielder, outfielder, switch-hitter, lawyer, and a founder of baseball's first players' union, The Brotherhood of Professional Base Ball Players, in 1879. Right, from the Baltimore Orioles' great 1890s team, a team heavy with Irish players: standing, Joe Kelley, John McGraw, unidentified; seated, Hughie Jennings, Wee Willie Keeler. Below, the Baltimore Orioles, pennant winners in 1894, 1895, 1896, surrounding manager Ned Hanlon.

Albert Spalding, as the senior states-
man and entrepreneur of baseball,
circa 1900. Below, The St. Louis
Browns, which won four straight
American Association pennants,
1885–88, and were Champions of the
World in 1886. Pictured below in
group photo in 1888, with the inspira-
tional player-manager Charles Comiskey
in the center. Overleaf: Players at the
Sphinx, during Al Spalding's baseball missionary effort to the world,
1889. The tour went to Hawaii, Aus-
tralia, New Zealand, Egypt, Italy,
France, and Britain, playing exhibition games. Spalding took it upon
himself to educate both royalty and the
crowds in the rules of the game—
doing a bit of marketing along the side
for his Spalding bats, balls, gloves,
and uniforms.

KING KELLY

"King Kel" could outdo any man moving from base to base or bar to bar. A five-foot-ten 185-pounder, Michael Joseph Kelly played from 1878 to 1893, primarily with the Chicago White Stockings and Boston Red Sox. He was one of the first great superstars in baseball history.

Chicago shocked the baseball world by selling Kelly to Boston in 1887 for the then unheard-of sum of $10,000. A lover of liquor, racehorses, and baseball, Kelly was an incredible and opportunistic competitor. Once he reportedly capitalized on a rule that enabled a substitute to enter a game at any time. As the batter swung at the ball, Kelly jumped off the dugout bench and screamed: "Kelly now catching." Then he smothered a foul pop-up that his team's regular catcher would never have reached.

Another time, in the bottom of the twelfth inning Kelly raced after a rising line drive. Leaping up in the distant recesses of the outfield, Kelly stuck his glove into the air and came trotting into the infield, ball in hand. The catch saved the game and his teammates were jubilant. "Nice catch, Kel," one of them shouted. "Not at all, not at all!" Kelly winked. " 'Twent a mile above my head."

The lively Irishman never feared to differ with other's opinions—even a private detective's report of his after-hours activity. "In that place," he told manager Cap Anson, "where the detective reports me as taking a lemonade at three A.M.—he's wrong. I never drank a lemonade at that hour in me life. It was straight whiskey."

Kelly owed a great deal to baseball, and baseball owed a great deal to Kelly. His daring base stealing and opportunistic play made the refrain "Slide, Kelly, slide," symbolize to multitudes just how exciting baseball could be. Once a laborer for three dollars a week in a paper mill, he earned $4,000 a season in the years 1887–1889. And he added to that income with stage appearances during the off-season. He was even an author, lending his name to *Play Ball*, a book that sold for twenty-five cents and was dedicated to the baseball players and fans of the United States.

His last major league season was 1893, when he was thirty-five years old. It was then that Kelly's longtime ambition to play for a New York team was realized—but only for a short while, for after playing in just a few games he was released, after which he toiled for a time in the minors.

In 1894 Kelly developed a bad cold that led to pneumonia. While he was being carried on a stretcher into Boston hospital, his bearers lost their footing and Kelly fell to the floor.

"That's my last slide," he quipped. It was. On November 8, 1894, King Kelly, whom Cap Anson once had characterized as "great a hitter as anyone," died at the age of thirty-six.

JOHN MCGRAW

John J. "Mugsy" McGraw was born on April 7, 1873, in tiny Truxton, New York, one of nine chil-

dren of a father who was a nine-dollar-a-week railroad man. When John McGraw was twelve years old,
his mother, stepsister, and three brothers died of
diphtheria. In 1891, shaped by hard times and trag-
edy, after stops in various minor league cities, the
five-foot-seven-inch 155-pound youth joined the Baltimore Orioles and became the toughest player on
what many deem the toughest team of all time.

The force behind three Baltimore pennants in
the 1890s, McGraw batted well over .300 from 1893
to 1900. Expert at the hit and run play, the feisty
infielder knew all the tricks of the game. He would
tag at a runner's shirt, belt, or pants to slow him
down. He would spike and bully umpires and rile up
crowds. He turned the hit and run play into his own
personal weapon. He would foul off pitches with an
ease that exasperated opponents—in that era foul
balls were not deemed strikes. Once he fouled fifteen
pitches in a row off Clark Griffith.

Feared, hated, criticized by the opposition,
McGraw played on in his own ferocious style year
after year, taking and giving no quarter. "I have
been trying to play ball," he defended his approach,
"for all there was in me to help my club win games.
This I will continue to do . . ."

KID NICHOLS

Seventh on the all-time list of most wins by a
pitcher, fourth in games started, and seventh in innings pitched, Charles Augustus ("Kid") Nichols
starred for Boston in the last decade of the nine-

teenth century, winning 25 or more games for five straight seasons.

One of the legendary workhorse pitchers, Nichols hurled more than 400 innings a year in each of his first five major league seasons. The Kid posted records of 30–11 and 29–12 in 1897 and 1898, leading the Boston Beaneaters to pennants both seasons.

At five feet ten and 180 pounds, the compact Nichols was able to deliver a moving fastball that was a major reason for his pitching success. His fifteen-year career ended in 1906, and he went on to managing. In 1949 Nichols was admitted to baseball's Hall of Fame.

JIM O'ROURKE

Jim O'Rourke was the man who recorded the first hit in major league history. In 1876, as a member of the Boston team, O'Rourke singled to left field with two outs in the first inning off Philadelphia's Lon Knight.

Dubbed "Orator Jim" because of his way with words, O'Rourke began his professional baseball career with Boston in 1873 in the National Association. It was there that manager Harry Wright suggested he change his name to conceal his Irish origins—at that time the Irish were not very popular in Boston. "Mr. Wright"—O'Rourke flashed the language that earned him his nickname—"I would rather die than give up my father's name. A million dollars would not tempt me."

One of the most popular players of his time, O'Rourke's lifetime batting average was .310. In 1945 he was inducted into the Hall of Fame.

OLD HOSS RADBOURN

The man they called Old Hoss, Charley Radbourn, piled up extraordinary pitching endurance records in the years 1881–1891. His specialty was hurling complete games—489 of them in his career, placing him seventh on the all-time list.

The 1884 season was his high-water mark. The Rochester, New York, native compiled a 60–12 record, striking out 411 batters in 679 innings as a member of Providence. In a stretch between August 7 and September 6, the Grays won 20 games in a row—and, astonishingly, all but 2 of the victories were accounted for by Radbourn. His salary for that momentous season performance was a meager $3,000.

A sturdy right-hander who developed his pitching skill on his family farm, Radbourn paid a hefty price for his professional hurling heroics. There were times when he was totally unable to raise his pitching arm above his ear. In Radbourn's time, players were their own trainers and healers, and the powerful pitcher had his own patented routine. Hot towels applied in relays to his abused muscles eased his pain. An iron ball flipped underhand by Radbourn was phase two of his special treatment. Then he would throw a baseball from three or four times the regulation pitching distance before a game, until he finally was ready to pitch again.

WILBERT ROBINSON

Born on June 2, 1863, in Bolton, Massachusetts, Wilbert Robinson's image and reputation in baseball lore derive from his deeds and misdeeds as a manager of some madcap Brooklyn teams. However, he was a fine baseball player in his own right, especially as a member of the Baltimore Orioles from 1892 to 1899.

On June 10, 1892, Robby came to bat seven times and recorded seven hits. He also batted in eleven runs as Baltimore romped over St. Louis 25–4. The daily newspapers the following day failed to make note of what Robinson had accomplished. It wasn't until two decades later that the famed sportswriter Heywood Broun publicized the event after learning about it in an offhand conversation with Robby.

Robinson was the team captain of the Orioles. Never a potent hitter, his prime value to the team was as an excellent handler of pitchers and as a defensive, durable catcher. His left "meat" hand had each finger broken at least once. His pinky finger's tip was amputated to stop blood poisoning from spreading to the rest of his body. The burly Robinson, according to reports of the time, looked upon the perils of catching in a matter-of-fact way.

"Aw shucks," he explained, "I'd go to bed with a lemon wrapped around the fingers that hurt," and be ready the next day.

90

AMOS RUSIE

New York City baseball fans have thrilled to the deeds of many top athletes; however, the first great sports hero in the Big Apple was the man they called the Hoosier Thunderbolt, Amos Rusie.

A powerfully formed right-handed pitcher, Rusie's speed and wildness were the stuff of legends. Five times he led the National League in walks, and he ranks fifth on the all-time list in that category. One of his high hard ones rendered Baltimore shortstop Hughie Jennings unconscious for almost four days. Another fastball came roaring back at Rusie off the bat of a hitter, smashed into the pitcher's ear, and caused him permanent hearing damage.

The success and the mystique of "the world's greatest pitcher," as he was known, was one of the reasons the pitching distance was moved from 50 feet to 60 feet 6 inches. Ironically, the change in distance, though it created more safety for batters, also increased success for Rusie, who was able to have more yardage for his breaking curveball.

From 1890 to 1898, Rusie averaged in excess of 20 wins a season except for 1896—that year he sat things out, protesting what he called "unjust fines" levied against him the year before. His status as a star pitcher was so elevated that, after much bickering, Rusie was able to sign a $3,000 contract for the 1897 season, the best season of his career—29 wins, 8 losses, best earned run average in the league.

ALBERT SPALDING

There is no telling how many records Albert
Goodwill Spalding might possess if he had not given
up his flourishing baseball career and decided to
concentrate his energies on his sporting goods business.

His stats boggle the mind: 47 wins, 13 losses, a
.783 percentage for the pennant-winning Chicago White
Stockings of 1876. A 56–4 record in 1875—the apex
season of his hurling the Boston Red Stockings to
four straight National Association championships.

Albert Goodwill Spalding was but seventeen years
old when he pitched the Forest City team of Rockford, Illinois, to victory over the Washington National baseball club. That performance transformed
Spalding into a national sports hero and served as
the first rung in a career that would make his name
synonymous with baseball as athlete and entrepreneur.

BOBBY WALLACE

Roderick John Wallace, better known as Bobby
Wallace, played in the major leagues for twenty-five
years—six of those years the last ones of the nineteenth century. His great claim to fame was revolu-
tionizing the way the position of shortstop was played.

Formerly a pitcher, an outfielder, a second baseman, a third baseman, Wallace was shifted to shortstop in 1899 as a member of the St. Louis team.

"Right off, I knew I had found my dish," he
recalled. Previously shortstops had fielded a ground

ball, straightened up, and then thrown the ball. Wallace innovated a new style—the scoop-and-toss.

"I noticed," he recalled, "more and more runners were beating out infield hoppers by a fraction of a second. It was apparent I had to learn to throw from the ankle and off balance as well." He learned well and in 1953 was the first American League shortstop to be elected to baseball's Hall of Fame.

JOHN MONTGOMERY WARD

One of the true superstars of early baseball, John Montgomery Ward was one of the most versatile figures of his time. The handsome Ward, a graduate of Columbia University Law School, was one of those who laid the groundwork for the Brotherhood of Professional Base Ball Players, which gave rise to the Players League.

From 1878 to 1882, Ward was a member of the Providence Grays, shuttling between the pitching mound, the infield, and the outfield. He won 87 games in 1879–1880.

Ward was traded to the New York Giants in 1883, and although his days of pitching effectiveness were behind him, he had many years of winning baseball left. He taught himself how to switch hit. And he taught himself how to steal bases, twice leading the league in that category. Ward even managed the Giants in the final 14 games of the 1884 season.

It was during his time with the Giants that he became one of the leaders in the Brotherhood—an odd role for one of the better paid players of his time, a figure who was married to a beautiful actress, a man who was the toast of New York City society.

Ward was a manager again from 1890–1894, but retired from baseball at age thirty-four to concentrate solely on his legal practice, which involved baseball players. Later on for a time he was part owner of the Boston Braves and throughout the rest of his life kept involved with baseball in some capacity. He died in Augusta, Georgia, in 1925 and was admitted to the Hall of Fame in 1964.

GEORGE WRIGHT

The star player on the fabled Cincinnati Red Stockings and the brother of manager Harry Wright, George Wright was one of those who revolutionized the way the position of shortstop was played. Placing himself deep on the infield instead of on the basepaths, as had previously been the style, Wright took advantage of his powerful arm to make the long throw to cut down a runner.

"George fielded hard-hit balls bare-handed," recalled his teammate Deacon White. "He gathered them up and speared them when in the air with either hand. He was an expert and accurate thrower, being able to throw with either hand."

From 1872 to 1875, George Wright teamed with his brother Harry to help Boston win four championships in the National Association. His last playing season was 1882, as a member of the Providence

94

Grays, the team he had managed to the pennant in 1879. Thus, in the space of eight years, Wright starred on seven championship teams.

With a partner, Wright organized the Wright and Ditson sporting goods business in 1871. It was a business that went on to enjoy international success. In 1884, the Wright and Ditson baseball was used as the official ball by the Union Association. Hall of Fame acceptance came to Wright in 1937, the year of his death.

HARRY WRIGHT

One of the most important figures in the long history of the national pastime, Harry Wright was known in some quarters as the "father of professional baseball."

The man who organized and led the fabled Cincinnati Red Stockings, Wright also inaugurated cooperative team play, hand signs for coaching, tours of foreign countries by baseball teams, and even knickers as part of a baseball uniform. He managed Boston to four straight pennants in the National Association—the first time this had ever been done by any team.

"Every magnate in the country is indebted to this man," the *Reach Guide* noted in 1896, a year after his death, "for the establishment of baseball as a business, and every patron for fulfilling him with a systematic recreation. Every player is indebted to him for inaugurating an occupation in which he gains

95

a livelihood, and the country at large for adding one more industry . . . to furnish employment."

Harry Wright, born in Sheffield, England, the son of a professional cricket player, was admitted to baseball's Hall of Fame in 1953.

CY YOUNG

The statistics compiled by Denton True Young in a fabled baseball career have earned him a reputation as one of the greatest pitchers of all time. A husky right-hander, Young began his major league career in 1890 as a member of the Cleveland Spiders and finished it in 1911. And when he was done he had won 511 games—more victories than any other pitcher in history.

The former Ohio farm boy's formal name was Denton True Young, but his nickname "Cy," short for "Cyclone," was apt. His fastball came up to the plate with blinding speed. Young posted 27 wins for Cleveland in his first full season and the following year won 36 games. In his twenty-two-year career Young won 20 games a season sixteen times, and five times won 30 games or more. He also recorded 3 no-hitters, including an 1897 gem over Cincinnati.

In the all-time rankings of pitchers, Young is first in wins (as well as losses), complete games, innings pitched. He is fourth in career shutouts and third in games appeared in.

IV
The Great Teams

THE CHICAGO WHITE STOCKINGS

Winners of the first pennant in National League history, the Chicago White Stockings won six pennants in the first eleven years of N.L. existence. The dominant team of the 1880s, the White Stockings posted a winning percentage of .636 over ten seasons. In the years 1880–1890, Chicago's lowest finish was fourth place. The White Stockings rolled to pennants in 1880, 1881, 1882, 1885, and 1886. They won 67 of 84 games, including 22 in a row, for a record percentage of .798 in 1880.

Driven by player-manager Adrian "Cap" Anson, who was not content for his team just to be the best in the National League, Chicago became a baseball team always on the move: Anson wanted his "Heroic Legion of Baseball" to be known as the best team anywhere. The White Stockings played exhibition games against all types of opposition in all types of settings.

It was a gala event for the small towns that were visited by Anson and his team. Sometimes Chicago players were outfitted in white stockings and Dutch pants. One season they were resplendent, dressed in white-bosomed shirts and dark dress suits. Traveling with a full entourage of helpers and hangers-on, the players arrived in the little hamlets of America seated in handsome open carriages drawn by white horses. And as the crowd assembled Anson in that booming voice of his gave the curious onlookers his patented pitch.

Connie Mack, who would go on to a fabled baseball career as player, manager, owner, recalled a visit by the Chicago team to his town of East Brookfield, Massachusetts, in 1883.

"We went over and looked over the sandlot where Anson's Chicago team was to play an exhibition game. It was a vacant lot littered with what I once called Irish confetti: tin cans, plug-tobacco tags . . . Some of the others and I were working in the shoe factory, and we used our lunch hours to dump the debris . . . from what we called the diamond. We wanted to get it out of our sight so that our Chicago visitors wouldn't stumble over it.

". . . The gala day in East Brookfield found all the villagers trying to see the game. It was a bigger event to us than the inauguration of a president. We cheered ourselves hoarse as Anson and [his team] trotted onto our sandlot. What a glorious sight it was. Anson played first base. A little fellow named Nichol

98

played in right field. What a roar he got from us East Brookfielders when he ran up behind the great Anson and sneaked between his legs! Cap, who was a born showman, appeared to be surprised and bewildered. We nearly burst our buttons with laughter at the spectacle.

"When it was over, we passed the hat to raise the $100 guarantee for our visitors. Dimes, nickels, and pennies fell into it. When we counted these we found we had just enough. With a rousing ovation from old East Brookfield, we waved our hats good-bye as Anson and his galloping Colts left our hometown."

Not all the Chicago games took place before overflow crowds. On September 27, 1881, the White Stockings of Chicago played against Troy, New York. The contest was meaningless—the Chicago team had locked up the pennant and Troy had a lock on mediocrity. The weather was miserable—it rained and rained. The only thing that made the contest memorable was the twelve fans in attendance: that wet dozen ranks as the smallest paid attendance in major league baseball history.

The innovator of spring training, the first pilot to coordinate infield and outfield play, the first manager to coach from the baselines and institute a pitching rotation, Cap Anson, at six feet two inches tall and more than 200 pounds, was a giant for those days. His creed echoed his feeling for power: "round up the strongest men who can knock a baseball the farthest the most often, put yourself on first base, and win."

The Chicago infield was known in the mid-1880s

as the "stone wall." Baseball's first superstar, player-manager Anson held down first base. Ned Williamson, "the greatest all around player the country ever saw," in Anson's phrase, was at third base. In a decade plus a year with Chicago, he batted .259, including 27 home runs in 1884, when what had formerly been ground rule doubles at Lake Front Stadium were counted as homers. Tommy Burns was the shortstop; second base was manned by Fred Pfeffer.

The outfield from 1880 to 1886 consisted of George Gore in center, Abner Dalrymple in left, and the illustrious Mike "King" Kelly in right field. Twice the flamboyant Kelly led the N.L. in batting and three times in runs scored.

Anson characterized Kelly "as great a hitter as anyone and as great a thrower, both from the catcher's position and the field, more men being thrown out by him than any other man."

However, it was the exuberant Kelly's base stealing dramatics that earned him his storied reputation. Kelly's version of the hook slide was encouraged by Anson and immortalized in the song "Slide, Kelly, Slide." The tune was sung with verve whenever Kelly reached base. And Kelly would launch himself head first, feet spread, toward second base, dramatically completing his run and slide with the tactic known as the Kelly spread.

William A. "Billy" Sunday was the team's utility outfielder from 1884 to 1887. Anson allegedly discovered Sunday in a race in Marshalltown, Iowa. In Anson's view, Sunday, who would go on to become a world-famed evangelist, "ran like a deer" and was the fastest man in baseball.

Frank "Old Silver" Flint handled the pitching staff. The catcher's mask troubled him ("I can't breathe with the damned thing"). Chicago pitchers included John Clarkson, who was admitted to the Baseball Hall of Fame in 1963. In 1885, his second year with the White Sox, the Massachusetts native won 53 games, including a no-hitter against Providence. In three full campaigns with Chicago, Clarkson averaged 268 strikeouts a season and compiled a won-lost record of 137–57.

Other star hurlers for "Anson's Athletes" included slow-ball pitcher Fred "Goldy" Goldsmith, winner of 98 games in his four full seasons with the Pale Hose; and Brooklyn-born Larry Corcoran, a hard-throwing right-hander who posted 3 no-hitters and a 190–83 record over five seasons with Chicago.

The Chicago team of 1882 was rated the best by King Kelly. "There were seven of us," he recalled. "Fred Pfeffer, the second baseman, could lay on his stomach and throw a ball a hundred yards. We wore silk stockings and the best uniforms money could buy. We had 'em whipped before we even threw a ball. We had 'em scared ter death."

That 1882 team destroyed Cleveland, 35–4, on July 24. Dalrymple, Kelly, Gore, Williamson, Burns, Flint, and Hugh Nichol each managed four hits to set a major league record.

In 1890 the Chicago team managed perhaps its finest moment. Racked by player desertions to the

Brotherhood League, Anson's roster was depleted of virtually all its regulars. Anson patched together a team he had picked up from the minors, from sandlots, from town teams. Fans called them Anson's Colts. Old Pop Anson batted .342 that year and marched Chicago to a second place finish just five games behind Brooklyn—a team that had sustained no losses to the renegade Brotherhood League.

Anson was forty years old in 1891 and was hitting slightly below .300. Writers suggested he might be better off if he retired. On September 4, the proud Anson played an entire game sporting fake whiskers in a not so covert mockery of his detractors.

The later decline of Anson as a player and various injuries to key Chicago stars finally brought White Stocking domination of the National League to an end. In 1897 Anson, playing in his last season, became the oldest player ever to hit .300. And on July 18 of that year he became the first major leaguer to collect 3,000 hits. The following season Anson was replaced as player-manager and an era ended. Chicago's new nickname was the Orphans—a tag that stayed with them through the rest of the nineteenth century.

THE PROVIDENCE GRAYS

A pennant winner in 1879 and 1884, the Providence Grays wound up in second place in the years in between and furnished spirited competition for the Chicago White Stockings. Managed by Harry Wright, the Grays boasted players who became baseball legends: John Montgomery Ward, George Wright, and Charles "Old Hoss" Radbourn.

Ward won 84 games for Providence in 1879–1880, including a perfect game against Buffalo. Radbourn was a one-man army in 1884, pitching Providence to the pennant, starting and finishing 73 of the Gray's 112 games, recording a 60–12 mark. His 441 strike-outs and almost 630 innings pitched led the league in those categories. The Old Hoss was rubber-armed and started 503 games during his illustrious career, completing all but 14 of them.

The spirited 1882 pennant competition between the White Stockings and Grays excited the world of nineteenth-century baseball and epitomized the rivalry between the two teams. Chicago trailed Providence by five games in late June, and its chances of repeating as pennant winners against a strong Providence team were considered slim; however, the Stockings swept the Grays in Chicago in mid-September before overflow crowds that milled about in the outfield grass as Corcoran and Goldsmith outpitched Ward and Radbourn. The sweep enabled Chicago to move on to win the pennant by three games.

THE NEW YORK GIANTS

Boasting a lineup that contained a half-dozen future Hall of Famers, the New York Giants won the National League pennant in 1888 and waged a furious fight for the flag against Chicago in 1885 and 1886. The nickname of the team originated in the 1880s when manager Jim Mutrie, commenting on the large size of his players and urging them on to victory during the course of a close game, bellowed: "My big fellows! My giants! We are the people!"

Mutrie's men included John Montgomery Ward, who came to the Giants from Providence in 1883; fiery William "Buck" Ewing, an Ohioan who recorded a better than .300 average in each of his seven seasons with the New Yorkers and earned $5,000 a year during the 1890s, the top salary of the time; James "Orator Jim" O'Rourke, an outfielder and sometimes infielder, sometimes catcher, who batted over .300 eight times in 19 seasons. And although overshadowed by Cap Anson, the Giant first baseman Roger Connor was a genuine star in his own right. And the following season, Connor notched a league record 17 home runs.

Right-hander Tim "Sir Timothy" Keefe, the premier hurler on the team, was 169–76 during his half decade with the Giants from 1885 to 1889. Keefe designed the uniform of the Giants—an all-black outfit with white lettering.

Michael "Smiling Mickey" Welch, a six-foot-three inch 190-pound southpaw, took turns as a starter for the New Yorkers along with Keefe. In 1885 Welch recorded 44 triumphs and a league-leading .800 winning percentage. Smiling Mickey Welch attributed the reason for his pitching success to his consumption of beer. "Pure elixir of malt and hops," he bragged. "Beats all the drugs and all the drops."

The Giants, with Welch and Keefe combining for

66 victories, battled the White Stockings for the National League pennant in 1885 down to the final days of the season. In a four-game series in Chicago before standing-room-only throngs of more than 10,000, the White Stockings won three of the four games.

The not-too-objective Chicago *Tribune*, comparing the differences between the two teams, observed that the crucial element was not speed nor brawn but "strategy . . . The White Stockings play a more brainy game."

The Gay Nineties saw a turn in the fortunes of the Giants as managers came and went. The saber-mustached Mutrie retired in 1891, and thirteen other pilots took a shot at directing the fortunes of the team. All these efforts were to no avail until John J. McGraw arrived on the scene in 1902 and brought back the glory days of the team.

THE ST. LOUIS BROWNS

The American Association Browns of St. Louis, owned by beer baron Chris Von der Ahe, managed four straight pennants 1885–1888 and second-place finishes in 1883 and 1889. Stars on the Browns included player-manager Charles Comiskey, Arlie Latham, Dave Foutz, and Bob Caruthers. To acquire Caruthers, Von der Ahe purchased the entire Minneapolis franchise, while the fee for Foutz, was the entire Bay City franchise.

Nicknames for the St. Louis players were not too complimentary but they were apt. Third baseman

Latham richly deserved the label "the Freshest Man on the Earth." At one point he had twenty postseason brawls scheduled—and five of those fistic encounters were slated against his own teammates. Pitcher Caruthers, the "Mighty Mite," was aptly tagged but seldom tagged by batters. Caruthers posted a 218–99 record for nine years through 1892, placing him first in winning percentage among all those hurlers who ever performed in the major leagues.

Charlie Comiskey, player-manager, built his team on solid baserunning, strong fielding, and brilliant pitching. The man they would call the Old Roman also viewed heckling the opposition as part of his team's game plan.

"About the toughest and roughest gang that ever struck this city is the nine of the St. Louis Club. Vile of speech, insolent in bearing . . . they set at defiance all rules, grossly insulting the umpire and exciting the wrath of the spectators." Oddly enough, that not too complimentary characterization was the observation of a St. Louis writer. Out-of-town journalists expressed earthier sentiments.

In 1892, after the American Association folded as a major league, the Browns returned to the National League. In the next seven years, Von der Ahe's men wound up twelfth in a twelve-team league twice and managed a fifth-place finish just once. Selling off stars and firing managers at a furious pace, "Der Poss Bresident" destroyed his entire winning and money-making operation. After the 1898 season the other National League owners had seen enough, and they forced Von der Ahe to sell out for the meager sum of $35,000. It is rumored that he muttered all that time: "Too late schmart."

THE BALTIMORE ORIOLES

The greatest team of its era was the 1890s Baltimore Orioles. Almost one-third of the major league players in the 1890s were Irish—a reflection of the immigrant waves that were swelling America. And the Orioles, too, were possessed of an Irish flavor: manager Ned Hanlon, John J. McGraw, Hughie Jennings, Wee Willie Keeler, Jack Doyle, Joe Kelley, among others.

The Orioles won pennants in the twelve-team National League in 1894, 1895, and 1896 and batted .332 as a team during that span of time. They finished in second place in '97 and '98.

"Oriole baseball" was tough baseball, innovative baseball, baseball of the next century: the hit and run, the backing up of throws, the positioning of players to take outfield relays. Baseballs hidden in the outfield grass miraculously appeared on cue in the glove of a Baltimore outfielder and an amazed batter would be held to a single—rarely more than that. On the basepaths wide hips and clenched fists characterized the spirit of the Orioles.

The lively Oriole team frequently started its practices at 8 A.M., and that was in an era when games began late in the afternoon. The time was well used as the Orioles refined their skills and readied their tricks.

Manager Ned Hanlon diligently drilled all his

Orioles in the fine art of bunting to capitalize on the rules change that had moved the pitcher's mound from 50 feet to 60 feet, 6 inches from the plate. And Hanlon instructed his grounds keeper to keep the grass growing high near the foul lines to help keep bunts in fair territory. The infield was also given special treatment. Kept rock-hard, that surface became the launching pad for the Baltimore chop. O's hitters smashed down hard on the ball, pounding it into the cement-hard infield, and scampered to first base before infielders could gather up the ball.

Fake throws, feigned steals, actual steals (six of the Baltimore regulars had 30 or more in '94), superbly executed cut-off plays—all of these had the Oriole opposition reeling.

"This isn't baseball they're playing," moaned Giant manager Monte Ward in 1894. "It's an entirely different game. I'm going to bring them up before league president Young."

A devil-may-care attitude and a legendary toughness were part of the Oriole way. Running down a long drive to the outfield fence, mashing his arm through the barbed wire, Willie Keeler still managed to make the catch and save a game against Washington even though he ripped his arm all the way up to his elbow.

The Orioles became known for "inside baseball." The tactic as applied to fielding was miraculous. When a ball was hit by an opposing batter, all the O's would shift gears and move about to new positions, depending on where the ball was hit. For example, if the ball was smacked to left field, the third baseman would race onto the outfield grass, positioned for a relay throw. Third base would be covered by the shortstop. The second baseman covered his own position. Backup coverage was provided by the catcher and pitcher for overthrows, while the center fielder also got into the act by moving closer to the left fielder in case of difficulty. The 1892 Orioles had committed 584 errors and posted the worst fielding average in the National League. The 1893 team with the new fielding approach at work reduced its errors to 293. And Baltimore leaped from a last-place finish in 1892 to a first-place finish in 1893. Oriole success was the final nail in the coffin of the 500-error season.

The 1894 Oriole season batting averages reveal just how powerful an attack the team was able to mount: McGraw, .340; Keller, .371; Kelley, .393; Brouthers, .347; Jennings, .332; Brodie, .369; Reitz, .309; and Robinson, .348. The Baltimore powerhouse won 24 of its last 25 games.

"We would have won all twenty-five," bellowed John J. McGraw, "if Robbie [Wilbert Robinson, the catcher] hadn't slipped going after a foul fly. The clumsy ox."

Robinson, the team captain, always claimed, "I was the soft soap artist of that crew. The umpires would call a close one against us, and somebody, usually McGraw, would come storming in." That would lead to violent protesting until Robinson would intervene and attempt to placate the umpire to prevent having McGraw or other irate Orioles ejected.

"Robinson was the sugar," cracked McGraw, "and I was the vinegar." Only once in his entire Baltimore career was Robinson tossed out of a game. After that he devoted his energies to maintaining his handlebar mustache and maximizing his baseball talent, which was as considerable as his growing girth.

One of the legendary stars of the Orioles was William Henry Keeler, but his short stature (five feet four inches) and slight weight (140 pounds) earned him the nickname Wee Willie. Keeler's bat was also undernourished, weighing just 30 ounces.

Keeler's greatest year was 1897, when he batted .432, recorded 243 hits, stole 64 bases, and scored 145 runs. In 1898 the left-handed bat magician collected 202 singles in 128 games—the most singles in a season by anyone who has ever played the game.

The most truculent of the Orioles was John J. "Mugsy" McGraw. Slapping the ball out of an infielder's glove, brandishing his well-sharpened spikes, switching baseballs in mid-play, berating and belittling umpires and opponents and opposing fans—all of these were part of McGraw's tricks of his trade.

One of the stars who was lost in the galaxy on the Orioles was Hughie Jennings. Acquired by Baltimore in 1893, Jennings was hobbled by a sore arm and played very little, managing to get into only 16 games. He sat on the bench and learned "inside baseball" from manager Ned Hanlon. And whenever he could, he nursed his arm in the warmth of a brick kiln. It must have helped, for from 1895 to 1897, Jennings batted .386, .398, and .355.

110

"Jennings, Kelley, Keeler, Robinson, and myself," McGraw mused, "organized ourselves into a sort of committee. We were scheming all the time for a new kind of stunt to pull. We met every night and talked over our successes and failures. We talked, lived, dreamed baseball."

THE BOSTON BEANEATERS

Up until 1887, the Boston National League team was known as the Red Stockings or Reds, but the Cincinnati team was the one most identified with the nickname. In 1887 the Hub club became known as the Beaneaters.

In the last quarter of the nineteenth century Boston finished on top of the National League eight times; however, the New Englanders really got it going in the 1890s—winning the pennant in 1891, 1892, 1893, 1897, and 1898.

The ace of the pitching staff during those glorious years in Boston was Charles "Kid" Nichols. During each of the pennant-winning seasons, the Kid won 29 or more games. Lacking a curveball, he utilized speed and control, working his trade off a smooth overhand delivery.

Nichols seemed always to have Baltimore's number. "You always know what the Kid is going to throw," complained Oriole manager Ned Hanlon, "but he beats you anyway."

Hugh Duffy supplied much of the punch for Boston. In 1888 Duffy had been a member of the White

Stockings, but Cap Anson was not enamored of him. "Hughie," Anson said, "you fall about five inches and twenty-five pounds short of major league size. The boys will eat you alive."

Duffy led the league in hits, doubles, home runs, runs batted in, and slugging percentage. Duffy and his outfield buddy Tom McCarthy formed the Boston tandem that was known as the Heavenly Twins. McCarthy earned a footnote in baseball history by prompting the rule change that governed when a player could leave a base after a fly ball was hit. McCarthy would allow the ball to hit in his glove and then juggle the ball as he raced into the infield. Only when he realized that it was impossible for a runner to advance would he cease and desist his juggling act and take full possession of the ball.

The Boston double-play combo for most of their winning years was Bobby Lowe and Herman "Germany" Long. Lowe lowered the boom on opposing pitchers one sunny afternoon at the Boston Congress Street Grounds in 1894. He bashed two third-inning home runs. Then he homered again in the fifth inning. Then he homered again in the sixth inning. The hometown crowd was agog—it was the first time in major league history that a player had homered four times in one game. The game was stopped and the jumping and jubilant fans rewarded Lowe with $160 worth of silver. In the eighth inning, all Lowe could muster was a single. And it is rumored that some of the disappointed fans wanted their money back.

The most disappointing season during the Gay Nineties for Boston fans was 1894—a year the

112

Beaneaters attempted to win their fourth straight pennant. Duffy batted .438, seven players scored more than a hundred runs, not once was the team shut out. Yet, when it was all over, Boston, who trailed Baltimore by just a half game heading into the final month of the season, faded and had to settle for a third-place finish.

One of the major reasons for the success of the Boston team was the braininess of its manager, taciturn Frank Selee, a tremendous judge of baseball talent—like Fred Tenney and Jimmie Collins. Both became fixtures at the corners for the last two Boston championship teams of the nineteenth century, in '97 and '98. First baseman Tenney came right off the campus of Brown University, while Collins was a graduate of the Buffalo, New York, sandlots. Seven straight seasons Tenney batted over .300. He originated the 3–6–3 double play and played wide and deep, foreshadowing the positioning of modern-day first basemen. Collins, innovator of the quick pickup and throw of slowly hit balls, is rated as one of the greatest third basemen of all time.

Poised for the twentieth century, Boston was a city and a team proud of its past—five pennants in eight years and eight pennants since the formation of the National League in 1876.

V
The Backdrop

BALL PARKS

The early environment of baseball games was that of a gentlemen's affair marked by the absence of spectators except for those invited by the teams. What spectators there were lolled about on the grass or sat on chairs or benches. The umpire was generally attired in tails and a tall black top hat, and in those early years he seated himself at a table along a baseline. Circa 1860, the general public became more and more involved as spectators, and winning replaced gentlemanly ways as baseball's operative factor.

The Cincinnati Red Stockings began play in 1876 in the National League in a ball park located in an area known as Chester Park. In order to get to the ball game, fans had to ride on special trains or in carriages. Crowds of 3,000 were common and considered a good payday for the team. When the National

League came into being, the White Stockings played their home games in a rickety wooden park on Dearborn between 23rd and 24th streets on Chicago's West Side.

During the 1880s and 1890s most parks were surrounded by wooden stands and a wooden fence. Some of the stands were partially protected by a roof, while others were simple wooden seats of sunbleached boards. That is how the word bleachers came to be. When those parks were filled to capacity, fans were allowed to stand around the infield or take up viewing perches in the far reaches of the outfield.

As late as 1900 some clubs even allowed fans to park their automobiles or carriages in the outfield. And in an 1897 game between Boston and Baltimore that drew more than 25,000 fans, the overflow crowd was permitted to stand just a few feet behind the infielders, creating a situation where any ball hit into the throng was ruled an automatic ground-rule double.

The environment at those games made it difficult for fans to follow the action clearly. Even though scorecards and programs were sold, no public address system existed, and there were no names or numbers on the players' uniforms.

Players were sometimes pressed into service to double as ticket takers. And during breaks in the action on the field, the dull moments were enlivened by the festive performances of brass bands.

Philadelphia, which had been expelled from the National League in 1876 when it refused to make a

115

final western swing, returned to the league in 1883, when successful sporting goods manufacturer Alfred A. Reach transferred the Worcester, Massachusetts, franchise to the City of Brotherly Love. The team played its games at Recreation Park, an irregular plot of land bordered by Columbia and Ridge avenues and 24th and 25th streets. However, the seating capacity of the park proved too small for the profits Reach sought. And on April 30, 1887, Huntington Grounds, a new Philadelphia park that seated 20,000, was opened. Distances were 335 in left field, 408 in center field, and 272 in right field. The center field section housed club offices and a swimming pool for players. The outfield contained a banked bicycle track that made outfielders huff and puff a bit going uphill after fly balls.

The St. Louis National League entry was known as the Browns and then the Perfectos—an odd name for a club with a not so perfect track record. The team left the National League twice, then returned and finished twelfth twice, eleventh three times, tenth once, ninth once, and once in fifth place in the years 1892–99. To attract customers to Robinson Field, St. Louis owner Chris Von der Ahe transformed his ball park into what he called "the Coney Island of the West." He installed chute-the-chutes (tubs that plunged with their riders into a pool), night horseracing, a Wild West show.

The popular tunes of the day were played by the Silver Cornet Band—an all-female aggregation

116

bedecked in long striped skirts and elegant blouses with leg-of-mutton sleeves and broad white sailor hats. In 1899 Von der Ahe changed the uniforms around in his zest for more color—the new garments featured red trim and red-striped stockings. The new uniforms brought new nicknames for the St. Louis team— Cardinals or Redbirds, they were called, and so they would remain.

John B. Day transferred the Troy National League franchise to New York in 1883; arrangements were made for games to be played on the polo field of James Gordon Bennett, publisher of the New York *Herald*. For most of the 1880s, the team played its games on a field at 110th Street and Fifth Avenue, across from Central Park's northeast corner. In 1899 the Giants moved to New York City plot 2106, lot 100, located between 155th and 157th streets at Eighth Avenue in upper Manhattan. The location was called "the new Polo Grounds," a horseshoe-shaped stadium with Coogan's Bluff on one side and the Harlem River on the other. The Polo Grounds seated 55,897, the most of any facility in the National League. A four-story, misshapen structure with seats close to the playing field and overhanging stands, it was an odd ball park that afforded fans the opportunity to be close to the action. There were 4,600 bleacher seats, 2,730 field boxes, 1,084 upper boxes, 5,138 upper reserved boxes, and 2,318 general admission seats. The majority of those who came to the Polo Grounds sat in the remaining lower general admission seats.

The visitors' bullpen was just a bench located in the boondocks of left center field. There was no shade from the sun for the visitors or protection from Giant fans who pelted opposing pitchers with pungent projectiles.

The upper left field deck hung over the lower deck; and it was virtually impossible for a fly ball to get into the lower deck because of the projection of the upper deck. The overhang triggered many arguments, for if a ball happened to graze the front of the overhang it was a home run. The double decks in right field were even. The short distances and the asymmetrical shape of the convoluted ball park resulted in drives rebounding off the right field and left field walls like billiard shots. And over the years hitters and fielders on the New York Giants familiar with the pool table walls of the ball park had a huge advantage over opposing teams.

Fires and progress would make steel and concrete replace the wood and timber of the nineteenth-century ball parks. The idiosyncratic dimensions of stadiums, the marching bands, even the real grass in many instances—all of these would ultimately become footnotes to baseball history.

UMPIRES

Mother, may I slug the umpire,
May I slug him right away?
So he cannot be here, Mother,
When the clubs begin to play?

Let me clasp his throat, dear Mother,
In a dear, delightful grip,
With one hand and with the other
Bat him several in the lip.

Let me climb his frame, dear Mother,
While the happy people shout:
I'll not kill him, dearest Mother,
I will only knock him out.

Let me mop the ground up, Mother,
With his person, dearest, do;
If the ground can stand it, Mother,
I don't see why you can't too.

Early umpires were selected from the assembled crowd or even from the ranks of players. They personified the amateur spirit of the game of baseball. And since it was an "honor" to be called to that task, the early umpires received no financial compensation for their duties. They wore whatever clothing they wished. Some of the more stylish early fellows showed up bedecked in Prince Albert coat, cane, top hat. They sat at a table or took up a stance or kneeled on a stool a brave distance from home plate along the first-base line.

The National League in 1878 revolutionized things by ruling that umpires would be paid five dollars a game and gave the arbiters the right to fine players up to twenty dollars for the use of foul language. Umps were also given the power to eject rowdy fans.

In 1879 the N.L. named twenty men whom it

119

deemed fit to be a cadre of umpires. For the sake of logistical convenience, the umpires chosen all lived in or close to cities where National League franchises were located. Prior to 1879, rival captains of teams had mutually agreed on whom they preferred to umpire a game. Now the league ruled that umpires could be chosen only from the select list of twenty men.

The gradually increased duties and independence of umpires were reflected in an 1882 ruling that abolished the practice of arbiters appealing to fans and players for guidance on a disputed play. Now umps were on their own to "call them as they saw them." And from 1882 on, all players except for the team captains were theoretically banned from engaging in any kind of menacing or meaningless banter with the umpire.

That 1882 season the American Association put in place a salaried staff of three umpires to be paid $140 a month. It was also the American Association that innovated clothing umps in blue caps and coats—a uniform that was aimed at giving the arbiters an air of respectability. Those uniforms were to become part of the folklore of the game—the dress code for the "men in blue."

In 1883 the National League copied the practice of the American Association, appointing four umpires for the season who drew salaries of $1,000 each. To ensure neutrality, to quell complaints that the new umps would not be political appointees, all the umpires were unknowns who came from cities that did not have National League franchises. The four men operated under trying conditions—serving without tenure, serving at the suffrage of the owners. Complaints by any four teams were grounds for the firing of any of the umpires, and not surprisingly just one of the four umpires made it through the entire season.

Changing rules, polemics in sports sections of newspapers criticizing umpires, the rugged nature of play—all of these made the work of the men in blue a tough task. Such terms as "daylight crime," "robbery," and "home umpire" were part of the lexicon of the times applied to the alleged foibles and flaws of arbiters.

In 1884 barbed wire was fastened around the field in Baltimore to contain the fans. That same season an umpire was beaten by an angry mob when he called a game a tie because of darkness. Police escorts were commonplace to move umpires out of ball parks and away from the menace of irate fans.

Dumping on the umpire was a practice encouraged by owners, who realized that fans howled in delight at the sight of authority being humiliated. "Fans who despise umpires," Albert Spalding noted, "are simply showing their democratic right to protest against tyranny." The protests pushed profits at the box office, and owners willingly paid fines meted out to players by umpires.

The system of two umpires working a game came into being in 1887 in postseason competition between the National League and the American Association. The first set of double officials was John Gaffney and John Kelley.

As a class those early arbiters were a colorful and tenacious group of men—they had to be, considering the not so genteel band of athletes they had to deal with. Umpire Billy McLean, who plied his trade in Boston and Providence, was a quick-triggered type. An ex-boxer, McLean kept himself in top physical condition; it was reported that he once arose at 4 A.M. and walked from his home in Boston to his umpiring job in Providence.

John Gaffney was called the king of umpires because of his longevity and resiliency. At one point, Gaffney was the highest-paid umpire, earning a salary of $2,500 plus expenses.

Bob Ferguson was another standout man in blue. "Umpiring always came as easy to me," he said, "as sleeping on a featherbed. Never change a decision, never stop to talk to a man. Make 'em play ball and keep their mouths shut, and never fear but the people will be on your side and you'll be called the king of umpires."

Tim Hurst, who coined the now-famous phrase about umpires, "The pay is good, and you can't beat the hours—three to five," was another of the fabled arbiters of nineteenth-century baseball. A rather smallish man who came out of the coal mining region of Pennsylvania, Hurst was quick-witted and quick-fisted.

In 1897 during the course of a game in Cincinnati, Hurst was struck in the face by a stein of beer that was hurled out of the stands. Hurst flung the stein back; it hit a spectator and knocked him out. A frenzied mob surged out onto the field heading for

122

Hurst. Policemen made contact with the umpire first. They charged him with assault and battery and arrested the irate Hurst, who was fined $100 and court costs by a judge.

Then there was the fracas in Washington in which Hurst mixed it up verbally with Pittsburgh's Pink Hawley, Jake Stenzel, and Denny Lyons. The quartet agreed to meet after the game to settle things once and for all.

Hurst went to work quickly. He punched Hawley in the face, smashed his foot into the shins of Lyons, and roughed up Stenzel.

"Timothy, what is all the excitement?" asked National League President Nick Young, who as it turned out just happened to be passing by.

"Somebody dropped a dollar bill, Uncle Nick," replied Hurst, "and I said it was mine."

"Oh, you're sure that's all?" asked Young. "It looked to me like there was some kind of a riot going on. Did the dollar bill really belong to you?"

"Not really. It belonged to Hawley, but these other two tried their best to take it away from him, and I wouldn't let them. It was just pink tea."

"Timothy, you did the right thing." Young smiled. "Now let's leave these follows alone. Come and take a walk with me."

Two umpires from that epoch went on to become National League presidents—John Heyder and Tom Lynch. Both men confessed to recurring nightmares of their time as umpires.

With all the pain and the abuse of the job

of umpiring, there were some redeeming aspects. The early umpires loved the game of baseball. They earned an average salary of $1,500 for seven months of employment, and as umpire Tim Hurst noted, it was a job where "you can't beat the hours."

In 1898 the Brush Resolution was passed, slightly improving the umpire's lot. John T. Brush, National League mogul, pushed owners into endorsing a twenty-one-point program to do away with the bullying of umpires. Expulsion for "villainously foul language" and umpire baiting were at the heart of the resolution.

The "purification plan" never worked and was ultimately given up as hopeless—no case ever reached the appointed discipline board, but it did raise the consciousness of the public, players, and writers about the plight of umpires forced to contend with the riotous behavior of scrappy and excitable players.

"Kill the Umpire" would be a phrase of symbolic import in the future—and that was a large step forward, for in the not so genteel days of the gilded age, that phrase had a darker and more sinister meaning.

EQUIPMENT

The evolution of baseball also saw a revolution in the type and amount of playing equipment. The day of purposeful—some would say superfluous—equipment, like the sweatband, headband, batting tee, batting glove, was far off in the future, but all equipment has its roots in the nineteenth century.

Bumps, bruises, and fractured fingers were part

of the lot of baseball players for years. The game was rough and tumble, the players were manly, and any type of protective garb was frowned upon.

Then one day in 1875, in a game against Boston, outfielder Charlie Waite of New Haven sauntered onto the field to play first base, his left hand adorned with an ordinary leather dress glove. The garment was an inconspicuous flesh color; Waite sought to attract as little attention as possible and did not wish to be considered less than manly by the partisans in the stands and his peers on the field.

Waite was able to glove his hand but unable to cover up what he was doing. The pioneer's "sissified" approach—the protective garment on his hand—triggered taunts and jeers from fans and players. Nevertheless, Waite played on, protected, swapping the pain of ridicule for the pain of a batted baseball.

One who always appreciated a good idea was Albert Spalding, a man who also knew too well the pain of a hard ball on bare hand. A year after Waite's glove appeared, Spalding and his brothers launched his sporting-goods business, a staple of which was the production of baseball gloves. And in 1877, when A.G. shifted from pitching to playing first base, he also shifted to wearing a glove.

"When I'd recalled that every ball pitched had to be returned, and that every hit one coming my way from fielders, outfielders, or hot from the bat must be caught and stopped, some idea may be gained of the punishment received," noted Spalding in defense of his wearing a glove.

The glove Spalding wore was padded but not

disguised in flesh color like Waite's; it was dark leather and there for all to see. "I found," explained Spalding, "that the glove, thin as it was, helped considerably. I inserted one pad after another, until a great deal of relief was afforded."

Spalding began the trend, and gloves began to catch on in all types of variations. Catcher Henry Fabian of New Orleans in 1880 utilized two gloves on his left hand and placed a piece of sheet lead between the surfaces. Cap Anson sported kid gloves with cut off fingertips on his throwing hand. Anson's catcher, Frank "Old Silver" Flint, got by with thin leather gloves cushioned with raw beef steak.

Actually the mouth protector, not the glove, was baseball's first bit of protective equipment. Sported by Cincinnati Reds shortstop George Wright in the 1860s, it was a patented piece of equipment and a welcome replacement for the broad rubber bands that had previously been worn around the mouth by catchers to save their teeth.

Wright's sporting-goods company patented, manufactured, and enjoyed some big-money days selling the mouth protector for a time, until it became a footnote to baseball history when it was replaced by the catcher's mask. As the story goes, the captain of the Harvard team, F. Winthrop Thayer, invented the mask, using the one employed in fencing as a prototype. He then presented the new model to his catcher, James Alexander Tyny, who had issued threats of quitting the game because of fear of disfiguring his face. Not until 1877 did professional catchers adopt the mask that fans referred to as a "bird cage" and that sportswriters ridiculed with such diatribes as: "There is a good deal of beastly humbug in contrivances to protect men from things that don't happen. There is about as much sense in putting a lightning rod on a catcher as a mask."

Despite the criticisms, sales of catcher's masks became a good business. Peck and Snyder's sporting-goods stores sold them for three dollars each. The store's ad copy claimed that "some of the top catchers of 1877" were using the equipment "made of wire and cushioned with soft leather . . . filled with best curled hair. They are light and easy to adjust."

Peck and Snyder of New York City not only carried the catcher's mask but also advertised "new styles of baseball uniforms and outfits; baseball caps, eight corners with star in top of corded seams for $10 per dozen ($1 sample by mail); uniform flannel for $8 a dozen, and second quality flannels at $6 a dozen." There were also belts for sixty cents each, heavy English all-worsted hose in either solids or stripes for $2.50 each or $27 for a dozen. With cotton feet, the hose were just $24 a dozen—three dollars less for leggings.

The real impetus making the catcher's mask an important part of the equipment of the national pastime took place in 1879, when the rules committee outlawed the foul-bound catch, banning catchers from retiring a batter on a foul tip caught on the first bounce. This change in rules made catchers play closer to the plate—increasing their chances of injury and increasing the need for protection.

More protection also came with the introduction of the chest protector, invented by a Hartford man as a way to eliminate the kayos of catchers who were laid low by foul balls pounding into their chest. Dubbed a sheepskin, the chest protector was placed under the uniform, but its bulging nature served as a magnet for boos. The first chest protector was allegedly employed by catcher John T. Clements of the Philadelphia Keystones in 1884.

By 1886 finger gloves were in fairly widespread use, and instead of two gloves most players now used only one. By the 1890s, gloves were standard equipment in baseball. A few players, like Fred Dunlap, however, went through their entire careers without ever using a glove. Dunlap claimed he didn't need "the thing," and maybe he was right. He led the National League four years in fielding in the 1880s sans glove. And there were others who, like Dunlap, could not give up the old bare-handed ways. "The game of baseball is being spoiled by allowing players to wear these abominations known as mitts," said Boston's Harry Schafer. "Players do not have to show skill in handling balls with those mitts in their hands. Those who cannot play without them should get out of the game and give way to those who can."

One player who benefited greatly from the use of a glove was Lave Cross, a massive catcher. Converted in 1892 to a third baseman when he joined Philadelphia, Cross played the hot corner buttressed by his catcher's mitt. Using his oversized glove like a fly swatter, Cross smacked down and snared virtually every ball hit his way. "They're playing infield with barn doors," some reporters complained.

In 1895 the rules committee came up with restrictions on "barn doors." All gloves except for catchers' and first basemen's were limited to no more than 10 ounces in weight and no more than 14 inches in circumference, as measured around the palm. The smaller glove was the end of the line for a few players, like Lave Cross, now unable just to hack away at fielding their position.

Baseball bats throughout history have possessed an almost mystical quality. Cap Anson allegedly hung bats like hams from the ceiling in the cellar of his house, and at peak times the old baseballer had at least five hundred pieces of favorite lumber seasoning away. Always on the prowl for a good piece of wood, Anson would go after ancient logs, shafts from carts, fence posts, anything he thought he could shape into good material for a baseball bat.

One of the more macabre stories about a baseball bat concerns a player named Perring, who, when the Ohio State Penitentiary was dismantled in 1880, collected the hickory wood that had formed the scaffolding that had outlived its usefulness. Perring fashioned the highly seasoned and strong wood into a bat that endured for the next two decades.

What would go down in legend as the famed Louisville Slugger, as the story goes, made its debut in 1884. Peter Browning, one of the premier batsmen of his time, broke his bat while performing for the Louisville baseball team. Faced with the pressure of a crucial game the following day, Browning prevailed on J. F. Hillerich at the local wood-turning shop to create another bat exactly like the one that had been broken. The day of the big game arrived. Hillerich had followed orders to the letter and presented Browning with a bat fashioned from the wood of a wagon tongue. Browning batted out four hits with that piece of lumber and Hillerich and Bradsby evolved into the leading manufacturer of the baseball bat—including the famed Louisville Slugger.

The baseball stems from the most primitive of beginnings. Albert Spalding, who would go on to make a fortune producing them, mused about his early experiences.

"The ball was not what would be called a National League ball, nowadays, but it served every purpose. It was usually made on the spot by some boy offering up his woolen socks as an oblation, and these were raveled and wound round a bullet, a handful of strips cut from a rubber overshoe, a piece of cork or almost anything, or nothing, when anything was not available. The winding of this ball was an art, and whoever could excel in this art was looked upon as a superior being. The ball must be a perfect sphere and the threads as regularly laid as the wire on a helix of a magnetic armature. When the winding was complete the surface of the ball was thoroughly sewed with a large needle and thread to prevent it from unwinding when a thread was cut."

The early baseballs had personalities all their

own. Their weights varied quite a bit—and a few of them barely tipped the scales at 3 ounces. Stitching sometimes consisted of crescent-shaped sections.

In 1877 the exclusive right to produce the National League baseball was granted to A. G. Spalding & Brothers. All the covers of all the balls were made of horsehide—an aspect of the ball that remained constant until 1973. Regulation and quality control, however, was an absent item as teams "ordered up" or "doctored up" balls to meet their own needs. The better fielding clubs utilized a soft ball, while those teams who had good hitters made sure the ball they used was hard and lively.

A baseball went through a great deal of heavy duty in those early years, unlike today, when it is routinely replaced for the slightest blemish. An outstanding example of the use and overuse of a baseball took place on August 7, 1882. The Cleveland Spiders and the New York Metropolitans played out their game in the rain at the Polo Grounds in New York City. The ball that was in use from the first pitch of the game was wet, soggy, and dirty. The ninth inning was under way and the captain of the Mets asked the umpire for a new ball to replace the virtually unusable and lopsided sphere. "I can't do it," said the umpire. "You'll have to play on with what you have." The arbiter's ruling was in the negative because the rules stated that a new ball could not be put in play except at the beginning of an inning. The ninth had begun.

UNIFORMS

We used no mattress on our hands,
No cage upon our face;
We stood right up and caught the ball
With courage and with grace.
　　　　　—George Ellard, catcher

The first "uniform," an outfit modeled after that of cricket players, was introduced by the Knickerbocker Baseball Club in 1851. The Knickerbockers wore straw hats, long blue woolen trousers, and white flannel shirts. Webbed belts held the entire uniform and the image together. By 1855 the straw hats were no longer on the scene—now replaced by flat-topped mohair caps, also standard cricket equipment.

In 1868, the Cincinnati Red Stockings introduced knee-length knickerbocker pants. Although the shortened pants spurred jeers from players and fans, the garment caught on, and today's baseball pants are in length modeled after them. The Red Stockings used cricket flannel and, to keep costs down, uniforms were ordered in just three basic sizes, so that a player could substitute for a worn-out uniform part quickly and economically.

A flashiness characterized those early uniformed teams as exemplified by the 1871 Athletics and the 1876 Louisville club. The Athletics were all the rage in white shirts and pants, blue caps and stockings. In 1876 Louisville players were a vision in white uniforms and caps, blue stockings, a two-toned belt, and

132

across their shirt fronts in navy blue in big letters the word "Louisville."

A more sedate look came to National League uniforms in 1878. As recommended by the Official Baseball Guide, the uniform was white and only one other color. In the view of the Guide that was the "prettiest" combination. The White Stockings of Chicago sported a different-colored cap according to a player's position. A. G. Spalding figured it would be easier for fans to pick out the players, and he also thought the different-colored haberdashery lent a touch of style to his team.

An altercation between Cap Anson and King Kelly revolutionized the style of belt loops. Kelly once snared Anson by his belt loop, preventing him from making a throw. Anson was so frustrated and angered by the incident that he prevailed on a sporting-goods maker to thread the belt through a pants' fabric and thus reduce the available surface an opponent could pull on.

Rules changes affected the look of uniforms. By 1882, the National League specified that a particular color be worn by each team. Actually white was mandated for belts, pants, and ties; the color of shirts and caps was determined by the position an athlete played. In 1883 lightweight silk stockings were all the vogue, and only the color of stockings was mandated by the league for each team. Oddly, when the 1899 season began, maroon stockings were worn by the Chicago White Stockings.

One of the more arresting, some would say funereal-looking, uniforms of nineteenth-century players was that worn by the New York Giants. Designed and sold to the team by pitcher Tim Keefe, the tight-fitting uniform was all black except for "New York" spelled out in white raised letters across the chest.

By the 1890s the quilted knickers of the decade before had been replaced by most teams who now wore comfortable uniforms made of flannel adorned with separate sliding pads. The total cost of these more "modern" uniforms was an expensive, for that time, fifty-six dollars.

As the nineteenth century gave way to the twentieth, numbers appeared on the backs of the uniforms of baseball players—an accommodation not to television or radio (that would come later), but to those business types who produced scorecards and wished to sell them to fans who could use them more pleasurably by being able to pick out the number of a player easily and thus keep a more accurate score.

Baseball shoes have undergone dramatic changes through the passing seasons. In 1877 the Harvard team replaced canvas shoes with leather ones that were laced around the ankles. More and more, high-topped shoes gave way to lower-cut ones designed to enhance a runner's speed. Spikes were in wide use by the late 1880s and also proved effective as an aid to a player's speed and traction.

Spikes also served another purpose—terror. "Give 'em steel," was the battle cry of Cleveland Spider manager Patsy Tebeau in the 1890s, "and plenty of it." The Spiders heeded Tebeau's advice and spent

134

hours sharpening and filing their spikes. They were not much as ballplayers, but the Spiders did terrorize the opposition for a time with their razor-sharp spikes.

In 1890 heel and toeplates, once sold individually, were collectively attached to the bottom of low-cut baseball shoes to enhance and improve a player's grip and traction.

By 1900 the look of the game, the style and the feel of uniforms had undergone radical changes in just a few short decades. And although the game of baseball would remain more or less the same, uniforms would be altered, adjusted, refined still more in the years of the twentieth century.

135

Epilogue

Now into its second century, baseball is still our national pastime. And the long legacy of those who played the game bare-handed on rutted fields in darkening daylight is still also a part of the game.

Baseball is still comforting regularity, a sport played and viewed from childhood on. It is still the individual battle of pitcher against batter, the movements of the fielders, adjusting, the signs relayed, received. Baseball is still shading, nuance, degree, foreshadowing, interval, climax. Its tempo is nineteenth century—prescribed by the game and not by the clock.

The season extends from the early green days of spring through the steam of summery nights and the blaze of August afternoons, into the bittersweet chill of the tenth month of the year—October. Half the time the games of a team are played at home; half the time the games of a team are played on the road. And

136

there is still time enough for rivalries to be renewed, for heroes to emerge.

The timeless ritual of the set lineup, the fixed positions, echoes back to baseball's beginnings. Four men in the infield, three men in the outfield, the pitcher throwing the ball on a white line to the plate, to the batter, to the catcher.

Baseball is the record of the program, the score-card, the yearbook, the line score. Baseball is the sound of the crack of the wood of the bat against the ball, the smack of the ball against the leather of the glove, the roar of the crowd, the rule of the umpire, the noise of the players.

Baseball is an evocation of another time, another century. The geometry of the diamond and the pastureland of the outfield play back the simple feel of an orderly, agrarian America.

Baseball's past is as real as its present, always close to the surface. Split images intertwine: Wee Willie Keeler and Pete Rose, John J. McGraw and Whitey Herzog, Cy Young and Nolan Ryan, Billy Hamilton and Vince Coleman, Dan Brouthers and Reggie Jackson . . .

Stats

NATIONAL LEAGUE PENNANT WINNERS

YEAR	CLUB	MANAGER	WON	LOST	PCT.
1876	Chicago	Albert G. Spalding	52	14	.788
1877	Boston	Harry Wright	31	17	.646
1878	Boston	Harry Wright	41	19	.683
1879	Providence	George Wright	55	23	.705
1880	Chicago	Adrian C. Anson	67	17	.798
1881	Chicago	Adrian C. Anson	56	28	.667
1882	Chicago	Adrian C. Anson	55	29	.655
1883	Boston	John F. Morrill	63	35	.643
1884	Providence	Frank C. Bancroft	84	28	.750
1885	Chicago	Adrian C. Anson	87	25	.777
1886	Chicago	Adrian C. Anson	90	34	.726
1887	Detroit	William H. Watkins	79	45	.637
1888	New York	James Mutrie	84	47	.641
1889	New York	James Mutrie	83	43	.659
1890	Brooklyn	William McGunnigle	86	43	.667
1891	Boston	Frank Selee	87	51	.630
1892	Boston	Frank Selee	102	48	.680
1893	Boston	Frank Selee	86	44	.662
1894	Baltimore	Edward H. Hanlon	89	39	.695
1895	Baltimore	Edward H. Hanlon	87	43	.669
1896	Baltimore	Edward H. Hanlon	90	39	.698
1897	Boston	Frank Selee	93	39	.705
1898	Boston	Frank Selee	102	47	.685
1899	Brooklyn	Edward H. Hanlon	88	42	.677
1900	Brooklyn	Edward H. Hanlon	82	54	.603

HOME RUN CHAMPIONS
National League

1876	George Hall, Philadelphia	5
1877	George Shaffer, Louisville	3
1878	Paul A. Hines, Providence	4
1879	Charles W. Jones, Boston	9
1880	James H. O'Rourke, Boston	6
	Harry D. Stovey, Worcester	6
1881	Dennis Brouthers, Buffalo	8
1882	George A. Wood, Detroit	7
1883	William Ewing, New York	10
1884	Edward N. Williamson, Chicago	27
1885	Abner F. Dalrymple, Chicago	11
1886	Arthur H. Richardson, Detroit	11
1887	Roger Connor, New York	17
	William S. O'Brien, Washington	17
1888	Roger Connor, New York	14
1889	Samuel L. Thompson, Philadelphia	20
1890	Thomas P. Burns, Brooklyn	13
	Michael J. Tiernan, New York	13
1891	Harry D. Stovey, Boston	16
	Michael J. Tiernan, New York	16
1892	James W. Holliday, Cincinnati	13
1893	Edward J. Delahanty, Philadelphia	19
1894	Hugh Duffy, Boston	18
	Robert L. Lowe, Boston	18
1895	William M. Joyce, Washington	17
1896	Edward J. Delahanty, Philadelphia	13
	Samuel L. Thompson, Philadelphia	13
1897	Napoleon Lajoie, Philadelphia	10
1898	James J. Collins, Boston	14
1899	John F. Freeman, Washington	25
1900	Herman C. Long, Boston	12

140

BATTING CHAMPIONS
National League

YEAR	PLAYER AND CLUB	GAMES	HITS	AVG.
1876	Roscoe C. Barnes, Chicago	66	138	.404
1877	James L. White, Boston	48	82	.385
1878	Abner F. Dalrymple, Milwaukee	60	95	.356
1879	Adrian C. Anson, Chicago	49	90	.407
1880	George F. Gore, Chicago	75	114	.365
1881	Adrian C. Anson, Chicago	84	137	.399
1882	Dennis Brouthers, Buffalo	84	129	.367
1883	Dennis Brouthers, Buffalo	97	156	.371
1884	James H. O'Rourke, Buffalo	104	157	.350
1885	Roger Connor, New York	110	169	.371
1886	Michael J. Kelly, Chicago	118	175	.388
1887	Adrian C. Anson, Chicago	122	224	.421
1888	Adrian C. Anson, Chicago	134	177	.343
1889	Dennis Brouthers, Boston	126	181	.373
1890	John W. Glasscock, New York	124	172	.336
1891	William R. Hamilton, Philadelphia	133	179	.338
1892	Dennis Brouthers, Brooklyn	152	197	.335
	Clarence A. Childs, Cleveland	144	185	.335
1893	Hugh Duffy, Boston	131	203	.378
1894	Hugh Duffy, Boston	124	236	.438
1895	Jesse C. Burkett, Cleveland	132	235	.423
1896	Jesse C. Burkett, Cleveland	133	240	.410
1897	William H. Keeler, Baltimore	128	243	.432
1898	William H. Keeler, Baltimore	128	214	.379
1899	Edward J. Delahanty, Philadelphia	145	234	.408
1900	John P. Wagner, Pittsburgh	134	201	.381

BASE STEALING CHAMPIONS
National League

1886	George Andrews, Philadelphia	56
1887	John M. Ward, New York	111
1888	William Hoy, Washington	82
1889	James Fogarty, Philadelphia	99
1890	Billy Hamilton, Philadelphia	102
1891	Billy Hamilton, Philadelphia	115
1892	John M. Ward, Brooklyn	94
1893	John M. Ward, New York	72
1894	Billy Hamilton, Philadelphia	99
1895	Billy Hamilton, Philadelphia	95
1896	Bill Lange, Chicago	100
1897	Bill Lange, Chicago	83
1898	Fred Clarke, Louisville	66
1899	Jimmy Sheckard, Baltimore	76
1900	James Barrett, Cincinnati	46

PITCHING CHAMPIONS
National League

		WON	LOST	PCT.
1876	A.G. Spalding, Chicago	47	14	.770
1877	Thomas Bond, Boston	31	17	.646
1878	Thomas Bond, Boston	40	19	.678
1879	John M. Ward, Providence	44	18	.710
1880	Fred Goldsmith, Chicago	22	3	.880
1881	Larry Corcoran, Chicago	31	14	.689
1882	Larry Corcoran, Chicago	27	13	.675
1883	Jim McCormick, Cleveland	27	13	.675
1884	Charles Radbourn, Providence	60	12	.833
1885	John Clarkson, Chicago	53	16	.768
1886	John Flynn, Chicago	24	6	.800
1887	Charles Getzein, Detroit	29	13	.690
1888	Tim Keefe, N. Y.	35	12	.745
1889	John Clarkson, Boston	48	19	.716
1890	Tom Lovett, Brooklyn	32	11	.744
1891	John Ewing, N. Y.	22	8	.733
1892	Cy Young, Cleveland	36	10	.783
1893	Henry Gastright, Pittsburgh-Boston	15	6	.714
1894	Jouett Meekin, N.Y.	35	11	.761
1895	Willie Hoffer, Baltimore	31	7	.816
1896	Willie Hoffer, Baltimore	26	7	.788
1897	Amos Rusie, N.Y.	28	8	.778
1898	Ed Lewis; Boston	25	8	.758
1899	Jay Hughes, Brooklyn	25	5	.833
1900	Joe McGinnity, Brooklyn	20	6	.769

Cited in the *Congressional Record* and honored by the New York State legislature as a sports historian, **Harvey Frommer** is the author of more than twenty books on sports, mainly on baseball. He was selected in a nationwide search to be the editor and principal author of the official book of the 1984 Olympics in Los Angeles, *The Games of the XXIIIrd Olympiad.* Frommer has a Ph.D. in Communications from New York University and teaches writing and speech courses in the City University of New York. He has just recently collaborated on autobiographies of both Red Holzman and Nolan Ryan.

WESTMAR COLLEGE LIBRARY

GV 863 .A1 F76 1988
Frommer, Harvey.
Primitive baseball
                        (88-1262)

≠ DEMCO ≠